THE JEWS IN CORDOBA
(X-XII centuries)

THE JEWS IN CORDOBA
(X-XII centuries)

by
Antonio Piñero Sáenz, Carlos Carrete Parrondo, María de los Angeles
Navarro Peiro, Jesús Peláez del Rosal, Angel Sáenz Badillos,
María Encarnación Varela Moreno, Fernando Díaz Esteban
and David Romano Ventura

coordinated by
JESUS PELAEZ DEL ROSAL

EDICIONES EL ALMENDRO
CORDOBA

First published by Ediciones El Almendro, Cordoba 1985, on the occasion of the 850th Anniversary of Maimonides' birth with the title: LOS JUDIOS EN CORDOBA (SS. X-XII).

Translated into English by Patricia A. Sneesby

© Jesús Peláez del Rosal

Ediciones EL ALMENDRO. El Almendro, 10 - 14006-CORDOBA. Tlfno. 957-274692

Cover: The statue of Maimonides in the Tiberiades Square in Cordoba's Jewish Quarter (Secilla-86) and an autograph page of Maimonides. (Commentary on the Mishna. Lenningrad Library).
Photos by Francisco González (Diario CORDOBA)

Reimpresión

Artes Gráficas Benzal, S. A. - Virtudes, 7 - 28010 Madrid
ISBN: 84-86077-48-6
Legal Deposit: M. 31.631.—1991

CONTENTS

PREFACE

In the elaboration of the proyect for the celebration of the 850th Anniversary of Maimonides' birth, the Organizing Committee did not hesitate to include in the programme of activities the series of lectures of the THIRD COURSE OF HEBREW CULTURE, which would take place in Cordoba during February and March, 1985, by outstanding specialists in medieval Spanish Judaism, from various Spanish Universities.

From the very beginning, the Organising Committee considered that, in order to examine Maimonides, the illustrious polygraph from Cordoba, the best way would not be through presenting him as an isolated figure but rather inserted within his time and context, among those who, like him, felt as much Jewish as Cordobese or Andalusian and who enjoyed the cultural privilege of living in Moslem Spain.

THE JEWS IN CORDOBA (X-XII centuries) studies the Golden Age in Spanish Judaism.

It is no exaggeration to say that it is impossible to understand Sephardism without knowing the history of the

7

Spanish Jews at that time. Cordoba was the birthplace of a cultural, literary, scientific and religious movement whose renovating legacy found its maximum representatives in men like Hasdai ibn Shaprut, Dunash ben Labrat, Menahem ben Saruq, Samuel ibn Nagrela ha-Nagid, Solomon ibn Gabirol, Joseph ibn Megas, Joseph ibn Saddiq, Joseph ibn Sahl, Judah Levi, Maimonides, and an abundant etcetera of Jews born, settled in or closely related to Cordoba.

This book broaches the study of those Spanish Jewish authors from different points of view -historical, literary, philological and biographical, which means that the reader will inevitably come across similar facts among its pages. Our first idea was to omit everything that might seem repetitive, but later we came to the conclusion that it would be better to maintain each chapter in its authors' original form, considering that this would contribute to the assimilation of the content and that repetition is one of the stepping stones in the learning process.

At the end of the book readers will found a Glossary of terms most frequently used.

JESUS PELAEZ DEL ROSAL
Director of the
COURSE OF HEBREW CULTURE

Introduction

JEWISH PRESENCE IN HISPANIA BEFORE THE TENTH CENTURY

by ANTONIO PIÑERO SAENZ*

1. THE JEWS COME TO HISPANIA

There is general agreement among researchers today that testimonies of Jewish presence in Hispania before Christ and during the first years of the Roman Empire are obscure and unreliable. In the Middle Ages Spanish Jews forged various legends claiming that their families had settled in the Peninsula centuries before Christ, probably with the intention not only of claiming a noble genealogy, but also of exonerating their ancestors of any connection whatsoever with the Christian Messiah's crucifiers.

But what can we really say about their presence? In the first book of Kings (IX,26) we read that Solomon's ships commerced together with those of King Hiran of Tyre. As the Phoenicians traded with the Far East as well as with many other lands, we can suppose that together with the Phoenicians some Hebrews settled on the peninsula coasts. Mentions in the Bible about trade with Tarshish (e.g. Is XXIII, I; Ps. XLVIII,8) used to be interpreted as references to Tartessus, the prosperous commercial area to the south of Iberia. Verse 20 from the prophet Abdias *(the exiles out of Jerusalem that are in Sepharad shall inherit the cities of Neguev)* has been taken since the Middle Ages as a clear reference to a Jewish diaspora in Hispania, bearing in mind that Sepharad has been the Jewish name for the peninsula since the times of Nebuchadnezzar's exile, six centuries before Christ. However, as we have already indicated, none of this

Professor of New Testament Language and Literature. Madrid Complutense University.

information stands firm as Tarshish probably refers in the Bible to a region in the Persian Gulf or in India, and Sepharad is the Hebrew name of a city in Asia Minor called Sardis in the 5th. century B.C., at which time Abdias' prophecy was composed. Therefore it can only be claimed with a certain amount of verosimilitude that perhaps. Hebrew traders had been coming to Spain together with the Phoenicians several centuries before the Christian era.

2. THE JEWS IN HISPANIA IN ROMAN TIMES

Modern historians consider that with all probability there were Jews in Spain before the 2nd. and 1st. centuries B.C. because of the mention of the Jewish diaspore in two passages in Strabo (geographer of the 1st. century B.C.) and Josephus (Jewish historian in the same century). Strabo tells us *"It is not easy to find a place in the inhabited parts of the world that have not received this people and been ruled by them"*. It also seems that Judas Maccabaeus in the 2nd. century B.C. might have had news of the conquests and fortune of the Romans in Hispania, and of their lust for gold and silver from letters sent from the peninsula by his fellow Romans (cf. 1 Mac. VIII,3).

The expansion of the Jewish areas in N. Africa since Helenistic times (3rd. century onwards) indicates the probability that some Hebrews crossed over to the prosperous Betica. There is evidence of Jewish expulsions from Rome and Italy as from 139 B.C., so it would not seem strange that many of the exiles sought refuge in the nearby Hispania. The Jewish catastrophe provoked in Palestine by Pompey (63 B.C.) and Titus (70 A.D.) with the taking of Jerusalem and consequent devastation of the country must have driven many Jews out of Palestine, and with all probability several families would have settled in the west of Spain.

Conjectures apart, what we do know for certain is of St. Paul's desire to come and preach the gospels in Hispania (Rom. XV,24-28). As this apostle always began his missions among the Jews, we can assume with complete confidence that in the 1st. century A.D. there were enough important

10

Jewish settlements in the peninsula to justify one of his journeys.

But it is not until the 2nd. century A.D. that we can find written evidence which offers no doubt whatsoever about the presence of a family of Palestine origin living in Hispania. This evidence is in the form of an epigraph in Merida of a certain *Justin*, born in Flavia Neapolis, (Siquen in the Bible), and today Palestinian Nablus. But what is not at all sure is that the Jewish inhabitants of Roman Hispania, republican or imperial, were descendants of the first Hebrews which might have settled on the Hispania coast under Phoenician protection. It would be wiser to suppose the contrary as after so many centuries and Judaism as yet with no models or organization, those first Hebrews undoubtedly would have failed to maintain their identity.

As far as the 4th. century A.D. is concerned, we have valuable documentation on the existence of a flourishing Jewish community in Hispania. We refer to decrees 16, 49, 50 and 78 of the Council of Elvira (near Granada, about 303-6) in which it is forbidden, under penalty of excommunication or other sanctions, that young Christians marry Jews, that the latter bless the fruits of land owned by Christians and that members of both communities sit together at the same table. Proved adultery of a Christian with a Jewish or Gentile woman was also severely punished.

From these coercive resolutions it is crystal clear that in the 4th. century a vigorous community of Jews existed in the south of the peninsula and that there was a great deal of contact between Jews and Christians, with the consequent danger of the latter having their faith contaminated by the opinions of the former.

For the 5th. century (418) we have a letter, written by Severus, Bishop of Majorca, in which he tells of the forced conversion of Jews in Menorca. In Mahon, instigated by the Bishop, a persecution of Israelites broke out which ended up in street fighting. The Christians set fire to the Synagogue and seized the Jews who were forced to convert or emigrate.Overwhelmed by the pressure, the head of the community,Theodore, forswore Judaism and another five hundred people followed his example. This gives us a clear

11

idea that the Menorcan Jewish group must have been prosperous.

ECONOMIC AND SOCIAL SITUATION OF THE JEWS IN ROMAN TIMES

What was the economic and social situation of the Jews in this Hispania, province of the Roman Empire? Unfortunately we have little news. What we do know is that there were Jewish settlements all along the Mediterranean coast from Ampurias to Malaga, and that they continued along the Atlantic coast as far as Cadiz and further. Inland we have documentary evidence of Jewish colonies in Lebrija, Seville,Carmona and Cordoba. In Lusitania, in Merida and Trujillo and to the north, in Zaragoza, Cuenca, Avila and Astorga. We do not know what kind of life they led but if it is true that the major part of these inhabitants came from forced emigrations from N. Africa, Italy or Palestine, we can assume that their living conditions were generally poor.

With the official conversion to Christianity on the part of the Empire, laws were passed as from Constantine's time which had a negative effect on the Jews, turning them into second class citizens. Constantine himself prohibited the Jews from owning Christian slaves, and obliged them to contribute towards the cost of the municipal courts, (they had been exempt up to that time). The emperors that followed confirmed these measures. Jewish tribunals also lost their special competences through Theodosius' successors and were gradually confined to purely religious cases. In this way the Jews became entirely subject to Roman law, instead of having their own legislation. Hispania, as one more province of the Empire, accepted precisely these laws which were unfavourable for the Jewish minority.

In spite of all this, it can be said that a certain amount of tolerance existed as we can deduce, for example,from the prosperity of the Menorcan community. One of its members, Cecilianus, enjoyed the title of defensor civitatis and another, Lectorius, had been governor of the province.In the times

12

before the barbarian invasions, when the process of economic ruralization was taking place, some Jews became landowners, and many others dedicated themselves, as *vilici* or *actores*, to administrating and managing the vast rural properties.

3. BARBARIAN INVASIONS. ARRIAN VISIGOTH REIGN

The invasions of the different groups of Vandals at the beginning of the 5th. century set in motion a series of calamities, killings and epidemics which affected the inhabitants of the peninsula, including the Jews. But these primitive invaders were soon driven south by the sweeping entrance of the Visigoths from western Germania, who came into the peninsula as confederates of the Roman Empire.These new invaders were merely a superstructure of nobles and soldiers and did not have much effect on the social organization of the Spanish Romans. They were too busy worrying about their own lack of stability, internal struggles and desire to firmly establish themselves to bother about the Jews, which meant a period of relative tolerance. The Visigoths were Arrian and the main problem facing their first monarchs was to stand up to the enormous Catholic majority over which they ruled. Nevertheless, among the laws passed at the beginning of the Visigoth rule some do include anti-Jewish regulations.

ALARIC'S "BREVIARY"

Alaric the second's code of law was called a "breviary" because it consisted of a selection from late Roman law,eliminating everything that was not suitable at that moment. This code maintained the exclusion of Jews from public office, repeated the prohibition on Israelites owning Christian slaves, and allowed any Christian to redeem a. slave of his own religion under Jewish ownership. Alaric also prohibited mixed marriages between Jews and Christians, the building of new synagogues (under a very severe fine) and that Jews unsettle their former countrymen who had converted to Christianity. As several researchers have pointed out, the object of this anti-Jewish legislation was to restrain the converting spirit of the Jews and so protect that of the Christians, all of which is an indirect indication of the solidarity of the Israelite community.

We can say little about the economic position of the Jews during this Visigoth-Arrian period. As the situation had changed very little, the Hebrews went on cultivating their own land or were helped by slaves. From time to time there is evidence of some Jewish craftsmen and of Jews who traded with different countries. What is really important, as Y.Baer points out (I,14), is that there is no sign as yet of any commercial development among the medieval Jews in Spain, although at this time there were visible signs of its commencement among the Jews in the Franco kingdom.

4.THE CATHOLIC VISIGOTH REIGN AND ANTIJEWISH LEGISLATION

This relatively peaceful situation was to suffer great changes when the Visigoths converted to Catholicism. This was due, undoubtedly, to political soon realised the need for unity and that different religions were a negative and diversifying element. It was inevitable that this way of thinking - together with other religious and apocalyptical ideas which we shall mention further on - would influence political and legal contemplations of that non-Catholic stronghold within the Visigoth kingdom - the Jews.

Recared, converted to Catholicism in 589, repeated the familiar prohibitions: the possession of Christian slaves by Jews and that public posts be occupied by members of the Israelite community. He also legalised the resolutions taken at the 3rd. Council of Toledo (canon XIV) which prohibited Jews from marrying Christians or having Christian concubines and determined the immediate baptism of the fruit of such unions.

14

In 612, when Sisebut came to the throne, the situation became much worse. As well as ratifying the decree then in force on the illicit possession of Christian slaves, in 615 or 616 Sisebut decreed that all Jews must convert to Christianity, a truly terrible measure that would even be rejected by Saint Isidore and the 4th. Council of Toledo (633). As a result, many Jews accepted baptism but many others decided to go into exile in the Franco province. The monarch's incredible obstination managed to obtain general forced conversions (remember those in Menorca in the 5th.century) which laid the foundations for a problem that was to afflict the Church in the future: cryptojudaism-Christians in name only who deep at heart carried on being Hebrews and practising their own faith. At the 4th. Council of Toledo, even though forced conversions were condemned as we have just seen, it was proclaimed that offspring of Jewish converts be separated from their parents and educated strictly in the Catholic faith. The old prohibitions against Jews holding public posts were now extended to converts.Sisenand, king in 633, approved - perhaps instigated - all these measures, so starting the custom of also discriminating politically against those already converted.

After a relatively quiet period, the virulent anti-Jewish legislation once again returned with Receswinth (653). Ten anti-Jewish laws were passed in his time as well as several council canons and a *placitum* - a written form of abjuration - which Toledo converts had to sign (654). These laws were directed as much against the converts as against real Jews;it was forbidden to celebrate the Passover, marry according to the traditional Jewish rites, practise circumcision, observe religious feasts and participate in lawsuits or any other activity directed against Christians. This load of prohibitions was enforced by severe penalties, death by lapidation or burning at the stake for retractors, that is to say, converts who reverted to Judaism, and other penalties against Christians who abetted Jews in the breaking of these severe laws.

After a short respite with Wamba, Erwig, his successor, passed twenty eight anti-Jewish laws in 681. Some of them are a repetition and reinforcement of Receswinth's legislation, with the addition of a few novelties. The penalties for celebrating the Passover or Sabbath became more varied and concrete, but he did eliminate the death penalty. Jews could not govern or punish Christians, they were forbidden to become managers of Christian estates and were pushed into forced conversion, with the consequent dilemma of converting or going into exile. But perhaps the most startling measures were the regulations affecting the control of the new converts' faith: they had to present themselves to the bishop or judge before undertaking a journey and on all Sabbath and other feast days. The idea was to prevent them from secretly attending religious celebrations. Very grave historical consequences were to come from the King's decision to entrust the cryptojudaism repression to the ecclesiastical authorities and not to a judge of law, as well as ordering that all documents concerning converts be kept in ecclesiastical archives. And so we have here as far back as the 7th. century the laying of the first stone of an inquisitorial bureaucracy that centuries later would be the Holy Office.

Erwig's successor. Egica, together with the 17th. Council of Toledo about 694, faced up to a presumable conspiracy on the part of Spanish Jews who, allied with other peoples from abroad, so it was said, were attacking the kingdom and the state as a whole. Researchers today agree on the actual existence of this conspiracy. In a brilliant article, Juan Gil has shown that towards the end of the 7th. century (about year 6000 after the creation of the world, according to Jewish calculations), the Jews throughout all the Mediterranean area went through a period of Messianic fervour. The terrible wars between the Eastern Empire - led by Heraclius - and the Persians, in the first decades of the7th. century, together with the double fall of Jerusalem,first to the Persians and then to the Byzantine Empire, led the Israelites to believe that they were witnessing the last battles, the final ones which were to precede the coming of the Messiah. In this atmosphere the Jews in Hispania had hatched a plot to rid them of the oppressive Visigoth yoke,trying to obtain support, not from those who would later become the Arab invaders in 711, as has been erroneously supposed, but from a tribe of Jewish religion in Magreb, the Berber Yerawas, who had been holding the Arabs in check in the north of Africa for some time. This conspiracy on the part of the Jews in Hispania is only one of many that broke out in the Mediterranean area at that time. So, faced with this threat, Egica and the Fathers at the 17th. Council of Toledo took terrible measures: all Jews - probably converts as well as non-converts - would be deprived of all their possessions, their families would be split up, they were condemned to perpetual slavery and forced to disperse to the four corners of the world.

These extreme and tragic measures were probably not carried out to their final consequences, as it appears that the successor to the throne, Witiza, was benevolent inmoderating their fulfillment.

THE ROLE OF THE CHURCH IN THE REPRESSION

In order to carry out part of their anti-Jewish policy, we have seen that the Visigoth kings made use of canons and resolutions taken by the Councils of Toledo, which means there was close collaboration between both authorities in this field. However, what is not at all clear is which of the two should receive historical credit for initiating the repressive measures. It seems clear enough in the case of Sisebut and Erwig that the monarchs themselves were responsible for proposing to the Church the ratification of an anti-Jewish legislation thought up by them. It is true, moreover, that the 4th. Council of Toledo frowned upon the forced conversions ordered by Sisebut, and that the 7th. Council was not exactly in favour of the anti-Semitic legislation promoted by Receswinth.

But, on the other hand, outstanding figures belonging to the Church in those times, like Braulius from Zaragoza, Julian and Ildephonse from Toledo and Isidore from Seville,wrote several tracts against the Jews and it is quite clear that the entire official ecclesiastical opinion had been prominently anti-Semitic since the Council of Elvira. Above all it is this negative religious atmosphere that leads the majority of researchers to the conclusion that the initiative

for the anti-Jewish policy can be firmly attributed t
Church.

JEWISH PERSECUTION AND THE VISIGOTH MONARCHS: CAUSI

Much has been speculated about what was behir
many laws against Abraham's descendants in the Catl
Visigoth kingdom. First of all it seems clear, in the ligl
García Iglesias' research that anti-semitism on the pai
the kings did not stem from social or economic causes,
from the desire to obtain easy money in taxes. And this,
the very sound reason that the public treasury was
especially benefited by these measures. Even in the extr
case of Erwig's laws, the property confiscated from the J
passed into Christian slaves' hands and these simply paid
same taxes as those applied to the origir
owners.Bachrach's purely political theory seems just as
unacceptable ; he attributes a harsh or lenient Jewish policy
to each Visigoth monarch coming to the throne corresponding
to the Jews' own attitude at that precise moment. Such a
theory cannot hold good, in the case of Receswinth, for
example,who was the son of a tolerant king, but nevertheless
himself a raging persecutor, but Wamba, his successor was,
on the other hand, tolerant.

It is certainly true that religious and political motives
lay behind the anti-Jewish measures; on the one hand the
Hebrews were the only religious minority that opposed the
crown's unifying efforts, on the other, the poor faith of many
Christians meant they were easily attracted to Judaism when
they observed the existence of a community utterly
convinced of their faith. The Church, if it managed to
convert that minority, would have eliminated serious
problems: it steered its flock away from the company
oferring sheep and obtained spiritual strength for believers.

Within this atmosphere of religious causes, we must
insist on the Messianic aspect. From J. Gil's research it is
evident that during the 7th. century the Mediterranean was a
religious boiling pot; many Christians believed the end of the
world was near, while the Jews awaited the coming of the

Messiah at the end of the century. Let us also remember that this was the century of the Mohammedan epoch. J. Gil uses solid arguments to attribute the forced conversion of the Jews ordered by Sisebut to his monolitical religiousness, as he was the most oriental of the Visigoth kings. When he heard of the fall of Jerusalem at Persian hands he thought the Anti-Christ has appeared. "If the end of the world was imminent the prophecy that the Hebrews would be converted by the end of the century must also be fulfilled. He, Sisebut,was the arm of the Lord to carry out what was written, that is, that those Jews..... should accept the true faith even if they had to be forced to, as the hour had come". Egica's terrible laws had had a similar motive, only on that occasion on the part of the Jews: the revolution and plotting against the State was caused by the belief that the Messiah was about to appear.

JEWISH SOCIAL AND ECONOMIC SITUATION BEFORE ISLAM. RELIGIOUS LIFE

The extension of the Jewish colonies in Visigoth times coincides to a great extent with that of Roman times, that is, the fringe bordering the Mediterranean and S. Atlantic.There were also some inland settlements as shown by somewhat more substantial documentary evidence. This evidence informs us of a great deal of Hebrew settlements, especially in Betica: Jaen, Andujar, Baeza, Cabra etc., cities with written evidence that Jews were living there, and yet no testimonies have appeared for earlier periods.

The few facts we have about Jewish economical and social life at this time confirm what we have already said: the Hebrews were neither all rich nor did they all dedicate themselves to trading and money-lending with high interests.It also seems clear that people had no general feeling against them, which explains the need for repeating the same anti-Jewish laws again and again, and they were never really complied with. We do know that both nobles and clergy were on good terms with the Jews and liked to make use of their services. On the other hand little conversion

19

could be expected to be done by a group that was detested and we have seen the need felt by the Councils to fight against this danger.

We can conclude from documents at that time that the economic conditions of the Jews varied greatly and we can find Israelites at all social levels. There is no evidence whatsoever of usury, but we do have proof that many were dealers without specifying a monopoly of any particular branch of commerce. Laws prohibiting the Jews, for example, from cultivating their land on Sundays shows us clearly that many of them were landowners. We also know that the continued administrating estates, as we have mention before.

In the same way references to Jews paying bribes avoid the application of laws against them and regulations about ownership of Christian slaves make it cl that many Jews enjoyed comfortable economic conditions. Israelite slaves also existed, some even with Jewish own or there would be no explanation for laws ordering freeing of slaves who converted to Christianism. There have been poor Jews too, as can be seen, for example, fro order issued by the Bishop of Merida, Massona, indic that in the charity hospitals founded by him, all poor p should be attended and no distinction made bet Christians and Jews. Semi-professional occupations, s silk-spinners, weavers, labourers with small holdi owners of some small craft business are all mentioned a number of times in laws. As can be appreciate varied picture has little in common with the topics use the Middle Ages when referring to Jewish economy.

As far as the Spanish Jews' religious life is conce can only presume that it was vigorous; the prob converts reverting to Jewish practices, the ardent desire for conversions, the prohibition on building new synagogues, the order to separate offspring from their parents in mixed marriages to avoid the contamination of a Jewish education, and the Messianic atmosphere already mentioned are all clear signs of a solid and fervent spiritual life. But we should not find this at all strange, as it is during the dark periods of religious persecutions that faith shines at its brightest.

5. JEWS IN MOSLEM SPAIN

EARLY TIMES

It is not to be wondered that after breathing such oppressive airs, Hispania should welcome the Arab invaders with open arms in 711. Like a trail of gunpowder the latest conquerors advanced to the north and, on the way, they left many cities with a garrison of Jews under orders to maintain control of what had been conquered. This gives us an idea of the extent to which the Hebrews cooperated with the new masters, taking revenge for past affronts. Perhaps for many sons of Abraham the coming of the Arabs meant the prelude to the period of Messianic liberation which, as we know, had bewitched so many minds towards the end of the previous century.

The situation slowly settled down, as the Arabs had at the beginning no intention of changing the Visigoth social and economic system. Then new families emigrated to the peninsula, especially from the north of Africa and the Mediterranean area, and even from Syria and Palestine. This period of honeymoon with their conquerors could not have lasted long as we have no evidence during the first part of Arab domination, up until the Caliphate, of Jews becoming extensive landowners or occupying important administrative posts. This was probably due to their not having converted to Islam. On the other hand we do have abundant evidence of the application of progressively heavier taxes to Jews and Christians living under Arab domination and of the arrogant and deprecatory attitude towards all non-Moslems. However, a more placid life with no specific persecutions or problems had succeeded the former period in the iron grip of the Visigoths. The new situation was to last more than eight generations and meant the longest lapse of time in all its history that a Jewish diaspore would enjoy with no problems in particular.

In 756 the period of *walis* or governors came to an end and the caliphate of Cordoba began, with Abd-ar-Rahman I,the outstanding young Ummayyad who had cleverly escaped from the Abbasids' killings. The Jews' keen nose soon led them to offering their services to the new caliph, so life pursued its normal course with no unexpected frights for the community. During his successor's reign, Hisham I (788-796), the dominant Islamic theology (that of the Malikites) tended to be harsh towards non-believers. But, even so, the potential danger never became a sad reality. The Jews, ever faithful, rendered important services to the dynasty but without holding as yet any prominent post in the Court, as can be seen from the records. During the reign of Al-Hakam I (792-822) we have concrete evidence that Jewish immigration to Spain continued.

In Abd-ar-Rahman the Second's time (822-852) there were several rebellions against the Caliph in the south of the Peninsula, in Toledo and in Merida, rebellions in which the Christian population took part. But there is no news of Jewish participation . Arab authors writing about this period invariably refer to the loyalty of the Jews, mentioning various tasks in which they collaborated with the government and presenting them under a favourable light. From 850-900 approximately, under Mohammed I, Al Mundhir and Abdullah, the caliphate seems to have suffered disturbances. But the Jews did not take part in these outbreaks either, not even in the famous revolt with Umar ben Hafsun, but we do have information that some Jewish families emigrated from the south to the new independent dominions, for example, to Badajoz or to Banu Kasis in Zaragoza.

Summing up then, until the brilliant times which were to commence in the tenth century with Abd-ar-Rahman III, the pacific existence of the Jews in Moslem Spain during the Ummayyads' reign, in Ashtor's opinion, should be taken both as a consequence of a tolerant policy on the part of the dynasty and of the attitude of the Jews themselves. They formed a group loyal to the government, a consolidated ethnic body which did not maintain any secret relations with elements outside the State that could cause preocupation to the governors. The Ummayyads needed people like these who depended voluntarily on them and lent them their support. The Ummayyads' enemies had disintegrating intentions, but the Jews' well-being required the existence of a strong central government.

JEWISH ECONOMIC ACTIVITIES UNDER THE FIRST UMMAYYADS

Once again we have the impression that although generally well-off, the Jews had not yet specialized in banking or trading, as would later be the case in the Middle Ages. As far as agriculture is concerned, we have already indicated that during the first two generations of the conquest the Jews had been almost completely unable to gain possession of any land as it was distributed among the new Arab masters,in the form of large estates. But in the 9th. century the continuous internal rebellions resulted in the necessary changes so that the land came under new owners, and among them, the Jews. Much land was sold and distributed by inheritance. On the other hand labour was cheap thanks to the flow of immigrants from the north of Africa, mostly Berbers. So the agricultural scene saw Jewish lords and peasants cultivating cereal crops, olive groves, orchards and vineyards. Our source of information is the questions on legal problems that the Jews asked their Rabbis and the written answers supplied. Many of these answers (responsa) referred to agricultural problems, especially in the Andalusian region.

In the same way we have responsa that mention problems faced by the Jewish handicraftsmen. It seems that the Jews carried out certain unpleasant manufacturing tasks that were repugnant to the Arabs, such as tanning and dyeing. And so a tradition was started that was to continue into the Middle Ages and is today recalled by street names, for example in Seville: Plaza de Curtidores y Zurradores (Tanners Square); Calle de los Tintes (Dye Street). The famous Cordovan leather work was already being produced and we know that Jewish handicraftsmen were also involved. This same industry was also famous in Zaragoza as we have news of Jewish shoe-makers there and also in Leon.

Another speciality in the south of Spain was silk production with Jewish participation. They almost formed a kind of monopoly in western Europe at that time and Cordoba and Merida were the two most important manufacturing centres.

Among the fine metal workers, silversmiths and jewellers, the Jews were particularly numerous. In Moslem Spain jewel-making was a tradition that had come with the invaders and immigrant Jews from the East had introduced Arab techniques and tastes which were apparently the most sought after by the rich Moslems.

Commerce increased during the Ummayyad period. Unfortunately we have very few references in the responsa although they are more numerous in the flourishing tenth century, which indicates that it was in this same century that Jewish merchants became prominent.

But before this, particularly in the 9th. century, we know that Jews took part in the silk trade and we have written evidence of jews participating in commercial traffic with the Northern Peninsula kingdoms and with the south of France. It seems that with in area in particular traders from the north of Africa (in Indian spices and luxury items) preferred overland routes across the peninsula avoiding commercial maritime routes which apparently offered more hazards. Within the peninsula itself cities as far apart as Lucena and Barcelona maintained continuous commercial contact, fundamentally Jewish, as it is well known that Lucena was inhabited almost exclusively by Israelites.

For the middle and end of the 9th. century we have a valuable document: *Book of Routes and Kingdoms* by the Arab historiogrpher Abul Kasim Abdala Ibn Kurdabeh, who was head of the Caliph's post service in the Media province. Writing about the roads and commercial routes of his time, he mentions a group of Jewish merchants, *Radanites,* who came from "the West" and spoke Arab, Persian, Greek,

Frank, Romance ("Hispano-Andaluz") and Slav. It is not clear whether they were from the south of Gaul or from Hispania. Probably the former, but they must have had a considerable number of agents among the peninsula Jews, the most famous representative being Abraham of Zaragoza. They used four routes, all of them from west to east or vice-versa, over land or by sea. One of the routes crossed the whole of the peninsula from north to south on the eastern side. According to Abul Kasim, the Radanite's commercial contacts spread as far as India and China where the Tang dynasty maintained the gates to the Empire wide open. It seems that the Radanites exported from Spain eunuchs, slaves, silk, furskins (brought from the north) and swords. From the East they transported luxury items and above all, spices. The golden age for this trade was indeed the 9th. century.

Slave traffic, precisely by the Jews, was also prosperous activity. These slaves mostly came from Slav countries, above all Yugoslavia, and they entered the Peninsula by way of the Frank territories. The governors of the south of Gaul did not worry too much about this type of trading, although it was absolutely forbidden that these slaves be Franks.Trade was prosperous until the Slav Orient was Christianized and in the end the Franks prohibited such traffic. Ibn Haukal and the geographer Al Mukadasi inform us that it was a flourishing trade in Spain and that the slaves acquired in this country were mostly from Galicia. The Jews from Lucena and other cities were very active in the 9th. century and a large proportion of slaves were castrated and sold as eunuchs.

JEWISH RELIGIOUS LIFE DURING THE FIRST CALIPHATE

During this quiet period Jewish religious life in the Peninsula also prospered. Talmud, universally recognized by the Jews, was the source of religion and education. The standard version that soon became valid in Spain was the Babylonian model and not the Palestinian one. We have evidence that rich and eminent Jews contributed economically so that copies of the Talmudical precepts could be acquired through trade with the north of Africa, and exact copies were made in the Peninsula. Eighteenth century scholars mention ancient texts which were meticulously published in Spain. Various sources indicate that modest academies dedicated to serious study of the *Torah* (the Law) had already begun to function in the eighteenth century, mostly in Andalusia. We have an indication in Cordoba of the high level of this circle in the literary discussion about the true Messiah between Pablo Alvar, one of the city's Christian leaders, and Rabbi Eliezer (a Frank converted to Judaism who had moved to Al-Andalus). This debate, held in Cordoba about 840-7, aroused considerable interest among the Christians and Jews from the city itself and the surrounding area, and its literary consequences have been conserved to our own day. Spanish Jews, however, recognised that the real experts on religious subjects were to be found in the theological academies in the Jewish quarter of Babylon, to be exact, in two cities already famous: Sura and Pumbedita. By way of N. African Jewish traders (mostly from Kairuan), Spanish Israelites sent written questions to the presidents (gaons) of these two academies. Authorized replies were required on legal and biblical queries that the experts in Hispania felt unable to pronounce on.

We have exact information that in 850 Lucena received a long reply from the president of the Sura Academy, and the Jews had been carrying out similar changes for several decades. As far as the Jewish community in Barcelona is concerned, we know that they maintained active religious correspondence of a legal nature with Amram bar Shesna, president of the Sura Academy from 858 to 871. In the second half of the century the Spanish Jews also established contact by letter with Pumbedita, and several of the responsa have survived. In payment and in order to maintain the Babylonian academies in general, donations in cash form were sent by Spanish Jews also by way of N. African traders. Around 775 a famous scholar, Natronai bar Habibai, who had tried unsuccessfully to become leader of the Babylonian Jews - move to Andalusia where his teachings on Talmudical matters were a great success audience-wise and he also committed to paper many that he knew by heart.

The 9th. century saw a growth and heightening in prestige of the rabbinical academy in Cordoba, so much so that questions begin to flow in directly. Among the Spanish Jewish scholars in the 10th. century Eleazar ben Samuel, from Lucena, author of numerous "responsa" became famous. Even so, he felt the need to perfect his knowledge at higher levels and he emigrated to Sura, taking an active part there in all activities concerned with the study and discussion of Jewish Law. His life clearly proves the strength of the ties between cultured Spanish Jews, fundamentally Andalusian, and the Jewish settlements in Babylon. It is curious to note, however, that in these exchanges Palestinian Judaism takes no part at all.

As the Talmud was too extensive Jewish judges and scholars felt the need to summarize the legal discussions in a kind of Code or Breviary. The most famous of these was the collection produced by Simeon Kayara from Sura about 824, titled *Ha-halakhot ha-gedolot* (The most important precepts). This Code circulated throughout the diaspore in two quite different editions. One of them enjoyed great diffusion among Jewish scholars between the 9th. and 13th. centuries; the one prepared in Spain in the 9th. century called "Principal Precepts *(halakhot)* in Spain".

As we can see, the literary facet of the Jews under early Moslem protection was mostly technical and scholarly and had not developed enough as yet so as to produce other purely literary creations. But the atmosphere was propitious and the necessary conditions of freedom, economic welfare and stability, forerunners to any creative literary impulse were well disposed for the brilliant period of Judaism which would flourish in the Hebrew culture in Spain in the follow-ing centuries.

Panoramic view of Cordoba's Mosque.

Judah Levi Square. Jewish Quarter. Cordoba.

Chapter 1

THE RENOVATING LEGACY
LEFT BY THE SPANISH JEWS

by CARLOS CARRETE PARRONDO*

The political map presented by the Iberian peninsula at the beginning of the 10th. century offers no complications whatsoever: the area extending from the south to well up into the Castillian plain (the river Tajo could mark the dividing line) was ruled by a firm caliphate authority seated in Cordoba, and it was enriched by a cultural level difficult to equal. The rest of the peninsula was made up of small Christian states still in process of formation, with a monastical culture and not a few internal conflicts: two peoples with different cultural legacies, of opposed religious ideas and different political mentalities.

Several Jewish communities were dotted about this ample geographical scene: Christianism and Islam had to live, for powerful historic reasons, side by side with the Jewish people dispersed about Sepharad. This situation was indeed to cause many problems, made even more difficult by the minority which also offered a millenary history, a religion revealed by one God, common to all, and a diaspore nearly ten centuries old. Characteristics that were certainly ambivalent and obtained very mixed results, as varied as that precise

*Professor of Hebrew Language and Literature. Salamanca Pontifical University.

29

geographical situation and historical moment in which the community's activities had to be carried out. Under the general term "community", with its many positive implications, are concealed very personal feelings of certain people who, in spite of their religious beliefs, reconcile as much marvelous collaboration as hidden malice. The Christian-Hebrew and Jewish-Arab relations must be considered, in any case, from a purely cultural point of view and not ethnical; the word racial must be eradicated once and for all from our text books (it is sometimes even found in more serious research) but this is not the moment for a closer examination even if it certainly is to suggest and disagree.

Some scholars, with very little accuracy but a certain amount of acceptance, try, with strict and obstinate delimitations, to differentiate between the historic areas belonging to the Christian, Arab and Jewish societies which would supposedly correspond to the centuries in question. And this is neither a true picture nor is it possible. Not even when, centuries later, there lived together in the Peninsula a cultural trio which were independent, autonomous , delimited and, nonetheless homogeneous, complementary and complete. This is the ideal way of looking at the social relations between the three communities.

1. JEWISH GOLDEN AGE: FROM THE CORDOBA CALIPHATE TO THE DISPERSAL OF THE EMPIRE

In Al-Andalus the first half of the tenth century is dominated by a remarkable figure: Abd-ar-rahman III (912-961) whose prolonged political activity can be summarized in two almost unrepeatable ideas: hierachy and culture, elevated to almost unsurmountable heights. In such favourable circumstances a unique figure appears - a cultured Jew, doctor, efficient administrator, translator of scientific tracts, diplomat and faithful servant to the reigning authority: Joshua Hasdai ibn Shaprut, founder of rabbinic teaching centres independent of the Eastern gaons. With him Spanish-'hebrew (to be more exact Hebrew-Andalusi) science came into its own, with loyal submission to the political authority under which it legally developed. Even admitting his outstanding personality, it would not be appropriate to consider him as a unique exception, but rather as a prototype naturally consequent to the living side by side directly, cordially (and with no indiscriminate proposals) of two ancient cultures. So Ibn Shaprut is like a mirror of the two societies, wavering on so many occasions but nevertheless called to a mutual understanding.

But at the beginning of the eleventh century a vital, heartrending event was to take place in the splendid Cordoba emirate: it was split into several factions, very often lacklustre, called Party Kingdoms and they marked the beginning of the fall of a brilliant empire. The first immediate consequence would be the gradual and progressive organization of the Christian kingdoms, conscious of the Moslem society's decadence and only too eager to assume a historic mission that they immediately considered a reconquest but, as far as the southern territories were concerned , was undoubtedly an invasion with no possible pretext on the grounds of historical revindications. And the Jewish people, strictly indifferent, although never mere spectators to these internal struggles, maintain a high cultural level, inheritance from their former contact with Islam. Two examples are the prosperous Jewish communities established in the Moslem kingdoms in Zaragoza and in Seville.

Not all the Party Kingdoms shared exactly the same characteristics of course. Those who, for historical reasons, proclaimed (or tried to) a secular aristocracy, ignored any collaboration from sources that were not purely Arab, so the Jews were left out of any reforming initiatives . But this was not the case in the kingdoms where the governors could be considered as coming very close to being tirants: obviously they would need a neutralizing force, objective too, capable of finding appropriate solutions and of carrying out unpopular measures; the Jews in this case played a fundamental role. When The enemy, (Christian or Moslem), threatened the unstable boundary limits, when an uncontrollable agitation was observed among the people and in short, when the necessary stability could not be guaranteed by those in power, then it was necessary to take firm measures, at the same time the most calculating, in order to try and quieten things down, at least for the moment. The Israelites would once again follow their historical destiny. In these circumstances, any sort of speculation could only be subjective. It is necessary to point out that the Jews in Al-Andalus took part in a critical situation with the sincere desire to collaborate with the Moslem population and institutions with which they had many bonds. It should not therefore be interpreted as a sign of revenge or of uncontrolled and extreme opportunism. According to history as it has reached us today, it is convenient to admit the sincere and conscious collaboration of the Israelite people in maintaining the Moslem authority when facing an enemy from the north, enemy which it considered as a real threat to its own identity as well.

SAMUEL HA-NAGID, GRANADA VIZIER AND PATRON TO THE ARTS

The figure, so often outstanding, of Samuel ibn Nagrella ha-Nagid (993-1056) is certainly representative of this loyal collaboration. From his native Cordoba, including Malaga and up to his settling definitely in Granada, his multiple activities -poet, patron, politician, vizier at the Granada Berber Court - there can be no comparison between him and the most eminent persons of his time. His war poems are undoubtedly perfect and never bettered, as has been shown by professor Angel Senz-Badillos, Professor on Hebrew language and literature at Granada University and expert on Hebrew-Andalusian grammarians and poets.

Very different from his father was Joseph ha-Nagid, autocrat, and also vizier of the Granada kingdom. Murdered in 1066, his sombre personality would represent the first signs of the termination of the repeated interventions on the part of Jewish personalities at the service of Moslem and Christian kings, participation that is fully documented for medieval Spain. It is what professor Haim Beinart from Jerusalem Hebrew University fittingly defines as a "Jewish Courtesan". The Jewish poets did indeed move in courtesan circles, adopting an Arab custom which, on close examination , presents two very different aspects; on the one hand the active presence of the Jews (and not only poets) in aristocratical palaces where there will soon be an abundance of patrons and the attractive cultural promises become eloquent realities, but on the other hand, and here is the danger. the influence of "Greek sciences" of rationalism and pleasure will lead to absence from the synagogues, forgetting the precepts of the Torah, which meant the disinte- gration of the social community and the appearance of religious heresy. It is lamentable that this was always present throughout the history of Judaism in its medieval diaspore.

The medieval Jew, interpreter of the Bible, was never first and foremost a theologian, as was usually the case with the Christian exegetes; above all he was a grammarian, philologist, scholar and expert on biblical science, the only procedure valid so as to be able to apply other auxiliary sciences as a consequence of the initial interpretation . The Andalusian school of Jewish grammarians was especially famous in what would be called today medieval Hebrew philology although its methods are a far cry from present day ideas. The grammarian exercised his science not only by composing extensive and reasoned vocabularies of Hebrew words and roots, but also discussing them in numerous biblical passages. Sometimes they moved right away from escolasticism and rigid erudition and used other more direct and lively methods: poetry, controversy, the literary style of responsa or questions and answers - high-flying diatribe. Cordoba was the centre of this brilliant school started in the tenth century and its caliphate court was a generous and impulsive host to this progressive initiative. Dunas ben Labrat and Menahem ben Saruq represented two different schools of thought and each took a hard line of argument in a confrontation with results which would give definite momentum to Hebrew grammar.

Born in Malaga but of a family originally from Cordoba, the poet Solomon ibn Gabirol (about 1020-1058) was an infatigable traveller throughout the Zaragoza and Granada kingdoms. It has been said of him, and correctly so, that he injected new vitality into Hebrew religious poetry; philosopher, satirical, forthright poet, all of these qualities combined in a sickly person who wrote such solid works as *Mibhar-ha-peninim* (Selection of Pearls), a fundamental book in Judaism; :*Keter Malkut* (Royal Crown), an extensive religious poem of unquestionable beauty, and a copious production of secular poetry.

Moses ben Maimon, Maimonides (1135-1204), is the most universal personality of the Jewish diaspore. RaMBaN, born in Cordoba, Talmudist, philosopher, exegist, doctor, lawyer and finaly encyclopaedian. But above all he was an authentic spiritual leader; his *Moreh Nebukhim* (Guide of the Perplexed) written for simple people, that is, the majority of the Jews spread about the diaspore, is the most representative of his creations. His incomparable greatness in every aspect persuades us not to fall into the trap of trying to capture his genial personality, but rather to regard him with the deepest respect.

2. THE CHRISTIAN KINGDOMS, AN EXPANDING FRONTIER

The Jewish communities within the territories of the Christian part of Spain, from the 10th. to the 13th. centuries, presented a very different picture to that of their neighbours in Al-Andalus. The cultural level was undoubtedly much lower; the beginning of its economy much more rudiment; civil legislation was only taking its first hesitant steps, and the Jewish communities were much more reduced and dispersed with only isolated and timid attempts at progress.

During the 10th. and 11th. centuries, the documentary evidence we have on the history of the Jews in Christian Spain is certainly scarce. We do know, from different documentary and epigraphical testimonies, of the existence of organized communities in the cities of Barcelona (several Jews perished in 985 when the city was taken by Almanzor), Estella, Najera, Castrojeriz, Celanova, Leon and Toledo after the reconquest in 1085. A dispersed population, impossible to determine its number, dedicated as we know to crafts and trade, but also, although some obstinately deny it, to agriculture. The eminently commercial picture of the Hispano Jew is valid but incomplete. The commercial activities , as well as other characteristics, form a mobile element and in certain circumstances show indifference towards problems that urban society had to face.

So far this traditional false picture of the Jew, only interested in increasing his personal wealth, fits in with the secular racial anti-Jewish feeling which unfortunately still exists in not a few strongholds within our modern society. But this idea is inexact - the Jews were also farmers and anyone who dedicates his life to cultivating the land, a noble and difficult task, shows at least a desire for continuance, for putting down roots, and a generosity handed down in silence to generations he will never know, and, finally, it represents a desire to defend something he will never surrender. Faced with the evidence of Jewish farmers in the Spanish diaspore, how can any vulgar theory be admitted in the sense that Jewish activities were exclusively directed towards his own personal benefit, ignoring the reality surrounding him? There can be no doubt about the answer; we must insist once more on the evidence that some people still refuse to admit: the Jew from Castile, Aragon, Navarra or Catalonia, and when applicable, from Andalusia, felt himself much more a native of that region than a Jew strictly speaking. Unless that reality is admitted on every side, we can advance very little in historic research. Another question altogether is that of considering the implications of religious motives, quite an important point but one that would require a different kind of analysis.

A testimony of special interest must be added to these precedents; the Castillian Jews, according to reports revealed up to the moment, were among the first authors of Castillian lyric poetry. When, at the end of the 11th. century, Judah Levi, one of the most famous Jewish bards, wanted to poetically consecrate Joseph ha Nassi Ferrizuel (Cidiellus), doctor and counselor to Alphonse VI, on the occasion of his visit to Guadalajara about 1091 to 1095, he wrote:

> *Des cuand mieu Cidyelo viénid*
> *¡tan buona albixara!*
> *com'rayo de sol éxid*
> *en Wad-al-jayara.*

which means:

> *The moment Cidiellus arrives*
> *What joyous tidings!*
> *Like a ray of sun shining*
> *In Guadalajara.*

It is a *khardja* a chant full of popular spontaneity, as was well shown by professor Francisco Cantera Burgos, from the Complutense University when, ten years ago, he collaborated in the publishing of an extensive if somewhat inconsistent study on the medieval Jewish quarters in the province of Guadalajara.

Judah Levi, perhaps the most universal of the Spanish Hebrew poets, was also attracted by the vigorous Andalusian culture. He moved from the northern Tudela to the south in order to frequent the literary circles under the shadow of Moses ibn Ezra. He became one of the most inspired Spanish Hebrew bards; his famous Zionides or his many religious compositions are only a sample of a magnificently terminated work of art. His life, however, did not follow the same vein; after his stay in Andalusia, he moved to Toledo and later set off for Palestine. Although a veil is drawn over his final years in which legend and reality create a total lack of certainty, it seems that he got no further than Egypt. Not a few of his compositions were incorporated into the synagogue liturgical chants and contributed to a great extent to unite, at a conflictive time when Jewish communities had to provide immediate and workable solutions to urgent and arduous problems.

In the Sepharad assemblies (aljamas), during certain critical periods, solutions were afforded, not by lawyers or autocrats, but by mystics and poets; we have here a detail, and not a trifling one, that should be taken into account once the moment arrives to look objectively at the medieval history of Spanish Jews, even if that moment is still far off. Poetical language, simple, unadorned (the poet always has something to say even if we do not want to listen), reaches people directly, the same as mysticism, uncomplicated by special language and full of inexpressible feeling. Legal language, on the other hand, needs an appropriate interpretation, and autocracy in any form can never be justified.

But the Jewish contingent, in many ways integrated with its neighbours, now Christian, did not limit themselves to enriching the poetical field only; there were also, as we have already seen in Al-Andalus, Jews serving the political authorities (Seset bar Solomon Perfet, dancer to the Catalonian Count Ramon Berenguer II is not an isolated case) or practising profane sciences, like Abraham bar Hiya, also Catalonian, astronomer and mathematician, author of the encyclopaedian work "Foundation of intelligence and tower of belief" which the late professor J.M. Millas Vallicrosa studied with rigour at Barcelona University more than thirty years ago.

A GRANADA ARISTOCRAT ON CASTILLIAN PATHS

At the beginning of the tenth century an event was to take place which was to shake the lives particularly of the Jewish communities established in Al-Andalus; the invasion of the Almoravides whose religious fanaticism would shake the very foundations of a society suffering so many years of a crisis which never came out into the open. The results are only too well known; a flow of Spanish Jews emigrating to the north, towards Christian Spain, to be absorbed into a society which they had not hesitated to label "barbarian" and correctly so, bearing in mind the cultural distance that separated them. And among the emigrants we find Moses ibn Ezra, the Granada poet who had conferred such great prestige on the refined literary circles of his native city. Now, with his family split up, a stranger in a land that had nothing to remind him of his far off Granada, living beside people so different to the Andalusian in the cultural field of his time, he could only lead a sad existence, roaming the lands of Castile and Aragon. How far away were the times when he could write so delightfully:

> My heart, my heart sighs for the gazelle;
> I loved her before she had being.
> Since the day she left, her eyes have tasted no sleep;
> They devote themselves to pasture the stars in the sky.

Nostalgy, loneliness, poetry, a moment of oblivion; we do not even have the tombstone of this stranger from Granada, lost in a land where he found no understanding.

ANDALUSIAN JEWS, TEACHERS IN THE CASTILLIAN ALJAMAS

This forced emigration of Andalusian Jews to Christian territories meant direct contact between two cultures physically close but opposed in so many aspects; this time the Andalusian Jew, on heading north, could only take in his hasty luggage one single offer, and it would take time for it to be accepted: his superior culture, at the beginning rejected but finally accepted if not fully assimilated.

Once the first Almoravide frenzy had settled down and under the indifferent gaze of the Christian society, The Jewish communities observed the radical collision between Christianism (Edom) and Islam (Ishmael), and they decided to offer their support to the Moslems as the only possible solution for keeping their millenary Messianic hope alive, and even of seeing it heightened. And here we have another premise that should be admitted in order to maintain the necessary objectiveness on examining the course of a threefold history. The Moslems, except on very few occasions, were - had to be - more generous and understand ing towards the Israelites than the Christians. The Moslems could really offer the Jews no more than the Christians, obstinate defenders of the advent of the Messiah come true in far off Palestine, more than ten centuries before, in the figure of Jesus of Nazareth. Undoubtedly here lies one of the initial causes of the polemical Jewish-Christian clash, so often absurd, and that would later develop into grotesque public confrontations (never dialogue) between both creeds, and the elaboration of not a few agreements, written with more passion than level headedness. They did not take the form of pointless discussions but of uncontrolled, spiteful exchanges, a long way from any objectiveness. The whole basis was false because faith rather, than convincing empirical demonstration, stems from a belief that is often blind but always noble and sincere; the opposite extreme is fanaticism and exaltation.

Faced with this new situation, sometimes hostile on the part of the dominant surroundings, the Jewish communities established in the increasingly solid kingdoms of Castile, Navarra and Aragon happily absorbed the traditional Talmudic rules which can be summarized as follows: the diaspore Jew must adapt to the civil legislation of the country in which he has settled; and he did so, living in unison and, moreover , contributing effectively so that the new legal measures could become effective calmly and in an atmosphere of normality and loyal spirit of collaboration.

The results were soon to come; in order to better the development of urban economy, the assembly (aljama) adopted for its social organization a structure parallel to the council established in the Christian cities and towns. We cannot refer (as is so often lightly done) to the non existent *imperium in imperio* on the part of a powerful social group challenging the legally constituted authority. Historical attitudes that belong to the nineteenth century, conventional theories and fictitious arguments should all be ignored; the Jews, as an organized community were eager to serve the royal power, and did so. The monarchy, seeing such loyal submission, recognized that the Jews belonged to the royal authority, a fact that during the centuries in question had special implications of recognition and protection. The Statute of Teruel (1176), foundation for diverse municipal legislation, states clearly that the Jews are the King's serfs and as such belong to the royal treasury. The Castillian courts, throughout the whole of the lower Middle Ages, ratified this statement, which would settle, sometimes even violently, certain pretensions on the part of people who tried to denounce or restrict public and community activities carried out by Castillian Jews. The Castillian Crown - let us bear this well in mind - was the greatest benefactor of the Jewish communities settled in Christian Spain (and also the most benefited). The expulsion edict signed centuries later, in 1492, by Isabel and Ferdinand, is not a contradiction of this fact. Are the reasons behind this drastic decision known in full detail? Has the part played by influential Jewish converts in this controversial document been closely examined? These, and many others, are the questions that need to be asked, but this is not the moment to begin a confused and perhaps controversial explanation.

3. ASHKENAZ AND SEPHARAD: STRICT ADHERENCE OPPOSED TO CREATIVITY

The second half of the 12th. century sees a period of Spanish Judaism impossible to understand unless we analyse the causes that made the pietists from central Europe intervene in the Jewish communities in Christian Spain. What some call French and German "pietism" (I ignore how far this term can be considered correct), should be interpreted as biblical, and particularly talmudical, rigour. And, above all, patrimony of the Asquenazi culture, conservative, in so many ways opposed to the freethinking, creative Sefardi. This is the moment when the confrontation will take place between two opposed, though not unreconcilable, cultural spheres. Asquenaz or centro-European Judaism and Sepharad or Spanish Judaism. The Spanish Jews, for many reasons (and not least of them precisely its geographical position, its unquestionable Arab influence and its traditional use of the Babylonian Talmud), were different to centro-European Jews

40

who were more traditional, with less licence on the part of the community, perhaps with greater orthodox strictness and with the Palestinian or Jerusalem version of the Talmud, the use of which might clear up many doubts that prevent us from understanding the tremendous cultural gap.

The Jewish leaders from central Europe observed with surprise and sometimes with indignation the literary and creative lines followed by their fellow believers in Sepharad; Averroeism could become a real threat to the pure mosaic doctrine; contact with Christians was a symptom of possible assimilation; the forsaking of synagogue prayer was striking at the very identity of the Israelite people; the extravagance displayed by some Jews went against a millenary tradition. The Asquenazs could not understand why a Hispano-Jewish simbiosis was taking place in Sepharad, in the same way that, earlier, Jews and Moslems had to a great extent come to live in unison. And so it was necessary to intervene and firmly; half way through the 12th. century important Asquenaz leaders moved to Toledo in order to review the legal and religious situation of the Jews in Christian Spain and to impose drastic measures, certainly unpopular, with the idea of avoiding possible irrevocable situations. The measures can be considered from many different angles: interference, autocracy, wise decision... The expulsion of the Jews from France was still recent and the controversy caused by Maimonides' renovating ideas at its height.

4. A FEW SUGGESTIONS FOR MANY CONCLUSIONS

We have here then an incomplete picture of the Jews established in Christian and Moslem kingdoms in Spain for three centuries. The picture offers, as well as others, the following suggestions:

- greater dynamism and higher cultural level in Al-Andalus, conveyor of a tradition superior to that of the Spanish Romans;

- steady progress of Hebrew grammar and biblical exegesis;

- unrivalled development of Hebrew poetry, with no possible comparison with any other community in the medieval diaspore;

- the polifacetical figure and immense works of Maimonides need no further comment than their own presentation.

- the mobile Christian-Moslem frontier meant living together and almost an assimilation of the population in the north of the Peninsula;

- Jewish cooperation with Moslem and Christian political authorities;

- drastic intervention on the part of Jewish leaders from central Europe to impede a process almost of self destruction ;

- protection of the Jewish communities established in their territories by the Monarchs of Castile and Aragon;

- renewing action by the Jewish poets and mystics contrary to the advocates of a traditional, conservative legislation and

- Sephardi Judaism puts down the roots of its authentic aristocracy in Spain, confirmed in the new diaspora in 1492 and still in existence with justified pride.

These brief considerations are neither suppositions nor wishful thinking, they correspond to an unquestionable reality. And the participation of the Andalusian spirit, on so many occasions very special and on so many others inexplicable, was even decisive on the occasion of the general expulsion ordered by Ferdinand and Isabel. Documentation preserved, although incomplete in many archives, shows that the Andalusian Jews - and what is more important, not a few Jewish converts - were important spiritual leaders of Castillian Jews and Judaizers during the final moments of their official presence in Sepharad lands. And their participation in Castillian arts, mysticism, "picaresca", and in general, in the fresh impulse of the Renaissance is a subject to be studied in due course, in its many attractive and fundamental aspects. But that is another question which I will leave to scholars who, with greater authority than mine, can provide a balanced and exact objective panorama which will perhaps coincide with the outline I have presented.

Chapter II

PANORAMA OF HISPANO-HEBREW LITERATURE

by MARIA DE LOS ANGELES NAVARRO PEIRO*

1. CULTURAL RENAISSANCE OF SPANISH JEWS

In the 10th. century a true renaissance of Hebrew culture took place in Spain and there is no doubt that Cordoba was the place where it originated. We could go even further and suggest that the Jewish cultural renaissance flourished in general throughout the Middle Ages. That is because, although there are important predecessors in the East like Saadia Gaon (882-942) - the most relevant author of the period called Gaonic, (from the end of the 6th. century to half-way through the 11th.), poet, exegist, talmudist, philosopher, translator of the Bible into Arab and the first grammarian strictly speaking - even so, it is in Spain where the range of Hebrew culture would open wide and include all the fields of medieval knowledge and literary art.

Several years ago, professor Perez Castro, reader of Post-biblical Hebrew Language and Literature at the Complutense University, described the characteristics of this period of Hebrew literature in the following words:

Professor of Hebrew Language and Literature. Madrid Complutense University.

43

"Although in the period of ancient history the literary production is, we could almost say, monochromatic, revolving round one single axis, religious, founded on and represented by the Old Testament, in the Middle Ages the picture is very different. We can distinguish as fresh characteristics its heterogeneous literary production, the individuality or personality we can observe, in contrast to the general anonymous character of ancient literary works, the interest in subjects outside purely religious limits:philosophy,sciences,interest in nature, the appreciation of the beauty of the world and of man, the value given to human emotions in liturgical and secular poetry, the interest in the possibility of harmony between religious or supra-rational matters and those scientific or merely rational, and so many others. Indeed in medieval Judaism all these features are to be found almost exclusively in Spanish-Hebrew culture... Spanish authors entered the field of secular culture with open minds, developing a real humanism with incomparable freshness. By the term "humanism" we only mean that Hispano-Hebrews were capable of developing all the possibilities contained within human feeling, spirit and intellect, without conditioning them by constraints and limits, and all this in Medieval times when other countries would earn themselves the general title of "The Dark Ages". These Spanish Hebrews were open to all the possibilities that man can offer, being forerunners by several centuries to what would later become known as Humanism with a capital H".

After enjoying this delightful description, let us take a brief look at the circumstances that favoured this amazing scientific and literary experience.

First of all we must emphasize the fact that the flourishing of Hebrew culture at this time is related to the political situation in general. The Caliphs Abd-ar-rahman II (912-961) and Al-Hakem II(961-976), managed to solve the internal conflicts that had troubled former reigns and establish a powerful and united kingdom. Cordoba became *dar-al-ulum* ("home of sciences") and its cultural level became famous in all

44

Europe. Artists and intellectuals gathered here from the furthest corners of the earth and Cordoba soon became the major cultural centre in the West, rivalling Baghdad in the East. Owing to the enormous scientific and literary advances on the part of the Arabs and the high cultural level attained by them, there is no doubt that the Jews who lived within this sphere enjoyed the possibilities of an education and access to knowledge that other commu- nities living in countries with a much lower cultural level lacked.

On the other hand, as far as literary art is concerned, we must bear in mind that the artistic wonders that the Arabs could do with their "sacred language" acted as a spur to the Hebrews. This was expressed by writers like Judah al-Harizi (XII-XIII) who, in an introductory chapter to his *Sepher Tahkemoni*, confessed to having felt induced to show the capacity of his "sacred language", in this case Hebrew, in rivalry with the language of the Arab writer Al-Hariri, whose collection of *Maqamas* - tales in rhyming prose interspersed with poems - had been translated by him into Hebrew. This was the reason why Al-Harizi composed the collection of Hebrew *Maqamas* known by the name of *Sepher Tahkemoni*, written also in rhyming prose with poems interspersed and with which the author makes a real display of knowledge and dominion of the Hebrew language. We shall insist further on this subject of rivalry between the "sacred languages" later, in another context.

Of great importance in the renaissance of the Hebrew culture in the 10th. century was the part played by Hasdai ibn Shaprut, doctor to the courts of Abd-ar-rahman III and Al-Hakem II. Hasdai reached a position of political relevance unequalled by any Jew up to that moment in Spain. Although it would appear that his main occupation was that of doctor to the Caliph, he also carried out other important functions. His knowledge of languages permitted him to successfully carry out diplomatic missions for the Cordoba Court, so his influence was also felt in Caliphate "foreign affairs". But what is most important in relation to the subject we are dealing with is his interest and intervention in scientific studies and his role as patron to literary figures of his time. Hasdai was considered as a *nasi* (prince) of the Jewish communities in Al-Andalus and contributed to a large extent, using his powerful means, to raise the cultural level of his people. He maintained relations with important Eastern talmudic schools and those in N. Africa, but his idea was to make Spanish Jews independent of subordination to the large Eastern centres. With this aim in mind he invited to Cordoba Spanish writers and scholars and others from outside the Peninsula. Hasdai's reception rooms were frequented by linguists, poets, critics and all kinds of scholars. Among his protegees were two of the principal Hispano-Hebrew poets. Dunash ben Labrat and Menahem ben Saruq, pioneers also in grammatical studies.

2. PRINCIPAL ANCIENT SOURCES OF INFORMATION
   ON THE LITERATURE OF THIS TIME

One very important source for investigators to reconstruct the life and literary production of medieval authors are the works of the writers themselves. In the books that have been conserved, there are facts about the life, historic and social conditions and even news of the writer in question or of his contemporaries. Thanks to these mentions we have learnt of compositions that have not reached us as they have been lost as time went by. On other occasions these facts are of great help in identifying works that were thought to be lost and have finally seen the light through the discovery of important manuscripts in the last two centuries. So, for example, the principal source of information about the life, political career and military successes of Samuel ibn Nagrella is his extensive collection of poems which re- flect the different situations, both physical and psychical that this prodigious figure suffered. At times and with all due respect it almost seems that we are reading some kind of personal diary where the author jotted down facts, thoughts and feelings.

Together with these occasional details, provided by the authors themselves, we have an extremely important literary source which supplies us with a great deal of information. This is the work of Moses ibn Ezra (XI-XII) *Kitab al-muhadara wa-l-mudakara* (Book of discourse and record), which we will refer to from now on simply as *Kitab*. This book, written in Arab, can be classified as a poetical precept and, in the words of its author, is: "A treaty which includes discourse (muhadara) and record (mudakara). It contains references to poetry and poets, aspects of techniques of prose and of prosists, a scattering of opinions from science and from scholars, testimonies of the words of pious and honest men, the latest news from philosophers and lawyers, flashes of important and famous men, a few paragraphs about the excellencies of writers and experts in rhetoric, phrases left by grammarians and scholars on religious questions".

From these words we can suppose that in this work the most varied subjects are touched upon, but, nevertheless, all of them have at least a certain relation to literary art. The author used the device of introducing different parts or chapters as if they were answers to questions posed by some speaker and for this reason these chapters are called "questions". The *Fifth Question* in this book replies to the question of why Spanish Israelites were superior to the rest of the Israelites in the composition of songs, poetical works and epistles. So this *Fifth Question* presents "the subject of the literary superiority in the Diaspore in Al-Andalus with an ordered and critical history of the different generations of grammarians. poets and learned men who succeeded each other right up to the author's contemporaries... Many of the names registered by Moses ibn Ezra are the only reference we have, but of many more, we have their works and collections of poems".

The *Fifth Question* begins by setting out the causes that explain the literary superiority of the Spanish Jews over those of other countries, and attributes this to being descendants of the tribes of Judah and Benjamin. But above all, to the profound knowledge of the Arab language. It refers later to the progress made by Hebraic grammar in Spain, and to how the patron Hasdai ibn Shaprut opens up a period of splendour in Hebraic literature in Spain. Moses ibn Ezra studies the different authors in chronological order, separating them into groups and generations, which he distinguishes by certain common features.

The information provided by this great work can be completed by other later sources, like chapters III and XVIII of

47

the book we have already referred to: *Sepher Tahkemoni* by Judah al-Harizi; these chapters are dedicated respectively to Hebrew poets in Spain and Hebrew poetry in general. The idea behind the book was different to that of Moses ibn Ezra. On the one hand, as we have already pointed out, Al-Harizi wanted to emulate in the Hebrew language the artistic and expressive achievements of works written in Arab; on the other hand, there is a clear intention of entertaining, amusing the reader with a series of stories around a protagonist who is a crafty vagabond, although educated and learned, with the fictitious name of *Heber the Kenite*. In each episode Herber shows a new facet or is disguised differently, so that not even his old friend who is telling the story can recognize him. This surprising character manages to fascinate his listeners with his speeches as he is an expert in oratory and he entertains them with his "experiences" and delightful stories.

The chapters in *Sepher Tahkemoni* referred to are introduced, the same as the rest of the book, as stories, but the moment the colourful protagonist begins to speak he shows his ample knowledge of literature. In chapter III the aim of Al-Harizi is to make a relation of Spanish-Hebrew poets and judge the fundamental features of their poetry; in chapter XVIII he prefers to present an overall vision of the different stages of Hebrew poetry in Spain, specifying the limits of a period of flourishment and another of decadence, mentioning exclusively poets he considers as pillars of Spanish-Hebrew poetry. In this chapter he also examines poetry composed by Jews living in other countries and his criticism is biting and destructive. For Al-Harizi, the same as for Moses ibn Ezra, the year 4700 after the creation - 940 in the Christian era - was a crucial moment with the appearance of Hasdai ibn Shaprut, who, with his patronage, encouraged poetical art among the Spanish Jews, and whose superiority Al-Harizi puts down to the fact of having inherited this art from the Arabs.

Although we must omit lesser relevant sources, for lack of space, we cannot fail to mention the information supplied by the historical work of Abraham ben David (XII): *Sepher ha-Qabbalah* (Book of tradition). Besides being a historian, Ben David was also a philosopher, physicist and astronomer. In his "Book of tradition" we can find important references to Hasdai's time, about Samuel ibn Nagrella, and other important figures as well as abundant details of the Andalusian Jews' exodus towards Christian states on fleeing from the Almohade invasion, etc.

3. FORMS OF LITERARY EXPRESSION

LANGUAGE

In the first place we must look at the language problem. What language did the Hispano Jews write in? We have seen that the two books mentioned before, the *Kitab* by Moses ibn Ezra and the *Sepher Tahkemoni* by Judah al-Harizi were written in Arab and in Hebrew respectively. Was it then a case of the author's whim in the choice of one language or the other or did certain conditioning circumstances influence the determination to use one in particular? In order to answer this question it is necessary to make another matter clear, that is, the language spoken by the Jews in the Middle Ages. Towards the end of the 2nd. century A.D. Hebrew was not used for speaking but survived in literature together with Aramaean for several centuries. Some authors, arguing that Jews from different countries made use of Hebrew in order to hold conversations or that on certain religious and political occasions it was used to safeguard the secrecy of what was said, defend the opinion that Hebrew has never failed to be a spoken language. However, the majority of researchers are of the opinion that from the end of the 2nd. century to the eighteenth, Hebrew is only a second language, not used for spoken communication, and it co-existed with the native languages spoken in the different countries where the Jews were living. With the Moslem conquests in the seventh and eighth centuries, a large part of the Jewish world was to accept Arab as its native tongue and was to live immersed in Arab culture.

What we do know for certain then, is that the Jews in Moslem Spain spoke Arab and wrote in Arab and also used Hebrew for certain compositions. From the works that have survived we can conclude that a great deal of prose was written in Arab and, on the contrary, poetry was composed almost exclusively in Hebrew. But why? The answer to this is not at all easy and some points are still obscure.

If we go back into the history of Hebrew literature we can see that, as from the second century when Hebrew was no longer spoken, religious rabbinical documents in prose were written in Hebrew and to a great extent in Aramaean - for example, the Talmud is written in Aramaean - while the religious-liturgical poetry, practically the only poetry cultivated by the Jews at this time, continued to be written in Hebrew. So a tradition existed among the Jews to versify in Hebrew, although in other kinds of writings the local language was used.

The primitive Hispano-Hebrew poets hesitated between using Arab poetical techniques, that is, its metre and verse, or continuing with the forms used in their ancient religious poetry. Finally the Arab forms were used, an innovation on the part of Dunash ben Labrat, but the language of poetry continued to be Hebrew.

The great linguist and dialectologist Yoshua Blau, a specialist in Jewish Arab, gives the following reasons to explain the use of Hebrew in poetry:

"Perhaps when the new poetic style appeared the custom of using Hebrew was so deeply rooted that it went on being used.... This use, however, was conditioned by the ideals of the new Jewish society that emerged in in Moslem Spain.... The Hispano-Hebrew poets were stimulated by their love of their sacred language and by the desire to envelop the most prominent expression of the new ideals of the Spanish Jewish society in the forms of their national language. They forsake the chance of reaching a wider Moslem public, because they considered that their mission was to serve their own Jewish society..

Hebrew poetry begins a new phase when it appears in Moslem Spain in the tenth century. As we have already said, Arab rules in versification were adopted in Hebrew verse. Arab metre based on quantity would be the dominant system in Spanish Hebrew poetry from the very beginning and right up to the expulsion of the Jews in the 15th. century. However, not all the poems written in Spain would follow Arab metre and versification; the tradition of the ancient liturgical poems would be conserved, particularly in religious poetry and we must insist that this religious poetry attained great heights, magnificent examples can be found translated into Spanish in professor Millas Vallicrosa's work: *La poesía sagrada hebraicoespañola* (Spanish-Hebrew sacred poetry).

But the most important innovation at this time was the appearance of secular poetry in Hebrew literature. Formerly, poetry had only been liturgical, with very few exceptions. In the new Jewish community in Moslem Spain, a community which prospered in the atmosphere of religious tolerance and wide ethnical and cultural variety, conditions were favourable for the birth of Hebrew secular poetry. This poetry absorbed the surrounding culture and developed rapidly under the Cordoba caliphate and the *Party Kingdoms* which appeared after its fall. Hebrew poets began writing, then, poems with very diverse content: panegyric, elegies, in self flattery, satire, songs in praise of wine, songs of love, of wisdom, of grievance etc., covering all the subjects of secular poetry.

Another event of importance in relation to poetical expression of this time is the revival of Biblical language which, in Spanish-Hebrew secular poetry, would substitute other linguistic circumstances that had occurred in Hebrew since the end of Biblical times. This return to the ancient sources of the Hebrew language meant an important innovation . Biblical Hebrew was considered as the only correct form of Hebrew, as a clear, precise and divine language of great beauty, superior to other languages. Such an attitude reflects the rivalry with the Arabs that we have already referred to, as the latter had converted the style of the Koran in a theological and aesthetical model. Although they wrote works in prose in the Arab used in Al-Andalus, everyday Arab, they made an effort to compose their poetry in the purest Koran Arab, classical Arab. The answer to this challenge lay in the adoption of Biblical style on the part of the Hebrews, a formidable opponent because of its antiquity and sacred character.

This is not the moment to go into details related to important aspects of poetry of this time, such as principle types of versification, the influence of popular Arabigo-Andalusian poetry etc., but readers interested in this subject can find ample information in the books available in English.

RHYMING PROSE

Spanish Jews also used this form of literary expression which, while sharing with poetry the adherence to metre and rhyme, is much less rigid in its application as the number of syllables is free, as are the length of the sentences and the regularity in rhyme change. Saadya Gaon, who we have mentioned as a precedent in the East as far as Spanish-Hebrew literature is concerned, had also used rhyming prose. But the novelty introduced by Spanish Jews was to write in the Hebrew language stories in rhyming prose in the style of the Arab *maqamas*. The *maqama* is usually an amusing tale, written in rhyming prose, interspersed with poems with metre and rhyme. In the *maqama* the writer puts special emphasis on stylistic brilliance, making use of rhetorical and literary figures, in a true show of linguistic virtuosity. This is a style we could call "baroque" in comparison with the more classical style of poetry of that period. The *maqama* can be classified as poetry although it contains elements of narrative prose. As a form of literary expression it began to be used by the Jews towards the end of the period we are discussing, the 12th. century. It is thought that the first *maqama* written in Spain was that of Solomon ibn Saqbel; little is known of him except that he appears to have lived in Moslem Spain during the first half of the 12th. century. His tale is set in a completely Arab atmosphere which reflects Moslem customs rather than Jewish. Nevertheless it is written in a language that is perfect Biblical Hebrew in its greater part and is full of rhetorical figures and play on words. We can also observe themes taken from Biblical literature, although the main subject is of Arab character. The principal work of this kind is *Sepher Tahkemoni* by Judah al-Harizi (XII-XIII) who we spoke of in the second part of this chapter. In a similar way to secular poetry, in the *maqama*, Arab forms were adopted, but the language used as a vehicle was Biblical Hebrew.

PROSE

Spanish Jews used the Arab language as much as Hebrew in prose writings. Arab was predominant in scientific tracts until about the 13th. century. The most famous poets, whose poems reached the highest level of perfection in the Hebrew language, wrote their prose in Arab. So, for example, the *Kitab* by Moses ibn Ezra, the *Kuzari* by Judah Levi, the philosophical works of Ibn Gabirol and the greater part of Maimonides' works were all written in Arab, although among the latter's works we can also find some written in Hebrew, such as his long code of law *Mishneh* Torah.

The fact that the Arabs, on writing prose, did not worry so much about the purity of the Koran language, as occurred in the case of poetry, and used the Al-Andalusian Arab, may have been one of the reasons why the rivalry that in poetry made the Jews try to attain the ideal of perfection in Biblical Hebrew did not extend to their prose. Another important factor in the use of Arab in prose was the penetration into fields which were new in Hebrew literature, such as philosophy, medicine, natural sciences etc., and Jewish authors had neither the terms nor the exactitude necessary for their works in Biblical Hebrew or in the later rabbinical language. For this reason even Hebrew grammar books are written in Arab, as happened in the important gramma- tical works of Hayyuy and Ibn Yanah.

The Hebrew that was used in prose was generally a mixture of Biblical and rabbinical-Talmudical language. It usually lacks the purity of poetical language and introduces neologisms and words borrowed from other languages, particularly Arab. In this case, as we have stated, there is no rivalry with Arab which led the writer to look for specially "pure" Hebrew, and the proportion of Biblical or rabbinical Hebrew varied from author to author.

4. PERIODS OF HEBREW LITERATURE IN MOSLEM SPAIN CENTURIES X-XII

Hebrew literature in Spain is usually divided into two periods: that of the Cordoba caliphate which corresponds to a period of initiation and renaissance and that of the *Party Kingdoms* which corresponds to a period of true development and splendour.

CALIPHATE TIMES (X CENTURY)

Let us see what the critic Moses ben Ezra has to say about this period, which we have outlined in the first part of this chapter:

> *After the Arabs became lords of Al-Andalus, conquering the Goths, the Israelites to be found in the peninsular,as time went by, learned the different branches of science from the Arabs. Thanks to their perseverance and assiduity in learning the Arab language, they were able to examine their works closely and penetrate the most intimate of their compositions; they became perfect scholars in the different scientific fields and at the same time delighted in the charm of their poetry. Afterwards,*

*God enabled them to understand the secrets of the Hebrew
language and grammar.*

So we have a stage of assimilation of Arab culture and of
formation in the different fields of knowledge. Innovations in
Hebrew literature are about to commence. It is a period of
trial, of first steps which will soon be consolidated and give
forth splendid fruits. We could also call this a period of
grammarians and poets, for it is in these two fields, grammar
and poetry, that the principal innovations are going to take
place and where we shall find the most outstanding figures.

We have already mentioned the first two Hispano-
Hebrew grammarians, Menahem ben Saruq and Dunash ben
Labrat, both protegees of the great patron Hasdai ibn Shaprut.
Menahem is the author of the first dictionary of the Hebrew
and Aramaean Biblical language, the *Mahberet*. Dunash, his
rival, wrote *Teshubot* (Replies) to Menahem in which he
criticised the former's work sharply and at the same time put
forward his grammatical theories on the Hebrew language.

This dispute filtered through to their respective disciples
and lasted for many years. Menahem never rose personally to
Dunash' attacks but a group of his disciples replied with the
Teshubot talmide Menahem (Replies from Menahem's
disciples) defending their master. It was Judah ben Seset, one
of Dunash' disciples, who wrote a further reply to this work,
also called Teshubot.

As poets of this generation, apart from Menahem and
Dunash, we must make particular mention of the following
figures:

- *Isaac ibn Capron* who lived in Cordoba in the second half of
the 10th. century. He also belonged to the group who
frequented Hasdai's reception rooms and as one of Menahem's
disciples he took part in the writing of the *Teshubot* against
Dunash.
- *Isaac ibn Mar Saul,* born in Lucena, one of the oldest Jewish
communities in Spain. Although few of his poems have been
conserved, we have evidence that he became famous not only
within Spain but also outside the Peninsula.

- *Joseph ibn Abitur* was born in Merida half-way through the tenth century but lived in Cordoba till 976, when he left Spain never to return. He travelled round several countries in the Middle East and according to the historian Abraham ben David, died in Damasco although we do not know the year of his death. He mostly composed sacred poetry in the old style and about three hundred of his religious poems have been conserved. Apart from his religious poetry, his best known composition is an elegy on the persecutions that took place in Palestine by order of the Egyptian sovereign, Al-Hakem, against non-Moslem subjects in 1012.

- *Isaac ibn Khalfun* was born in Spain or N. Africa half-way through the tenth century. He lived for some time in Cordoba but mostly wandered from place to place; he was the first roving bard in Hebrew literature and Moses ibn Ezra says of him:

> *None among the Jewish poets was prepared to take up poetry as a profession, nor chose to write verses as a means of earning his living, only he, who made use of and roamed the world with his poetry, obtaining from generous people the good things he desired.*

So he has abundant works of praise and panegyric, as they enabled him to earn his living.

FALL OF THE CALIPHATE

Hisham II, successor to Al-Hakem II, inherited neither the qualities nor the interest in government that his predecessor had shown and handed the power over to his favourites. The stability of the caliphate was conserved at first because of his prime minister Almanzor, who, thanks to his own merits and the patronage of the Caliph's mother, took over the reigns of government. He was the person who really ruled the caliphate at this time and it was certainly the greatest period of power and military splendour. When Almanzor died, he was succeeded by his son Muzaffar who, although not up to the same level as his father, was worthy of him, but this was not the case when, on his death, his brother Sanchuelo took over as the third regent to Caliph Hisham II. Sanchuelo committed mistake after mistake, the greatest of them being the pretension to having descended from royalty. He had Hisham name him as successor to the throne and this provoked indignation and rebellion among the many direct descendants to Abd-ar-Rahman III, who considered themselves robbed of their legitimate rights. This reaction found support among the people of Cordoba and in 1009 the Cordoba rebellion broke out. Sanchuelo was defeated and killed. Anarchy was the result and for twenty years there was a rapid succession of caliphs. Finally the last Ummayyad caliph, Hisham III, was forced to abdicate in 1031.

Let us look now at the way Moses ibn Ezra describes the step from the previous literary generation to the one we are interested in:

... *Later, in Al-Andalus the senseless and terrible revolution took place, called the Berber rebellion, at the end of the aforesaid century. There was an increase in all sorts of disasters, the calamities of the world became immense and need became more rife in the country, emigration multiplied among the subjects and the seat of the principality and capital, Cordoba, suffered all sorts of strange misfortunes: it fell into ruins, or almost. Sciences were weakened by the exodus and because people were so busy with such disastrous times. Finally, this penury came to an end and this drowning people could breathe again. This generation was succeeded by another, whose words were sweeter and whose intentions and aims gentler.*

PERIOD OF THE PARTY KINGDOMS

Moslem power had benn divided and small states called Party Kingdoms were flourishing. Although the founding of these *kingdoms* meant a decisive change in the development of

Spanish Moslem history and was accompanied by a rupture in political and social continuity, the new governors made a great effort to imitate the ways and customs of the Ummayyad caliphs, but their greatest effort went into surpassing the luxury and splendour of the Baghdad Court and Baghdad fashions were followed in customs and ceremonies. Many of the minor kings did all they could to endow their courts with a high cultural level and they certainly tried to turn them into centres of literary creation. Consequently they never hesitated in favouring and protecting Jews who showed talent.

This was the beginning of a period in the life of Jews in Moslem Spain that historians have called the "Golden Age". The atmosphere in these kingdoms was generally of religious tolerance and of a certain relaxation in customs. So, for example, philosophical studies, which had been so persecuted by Almanzor, were well received by the kings and philosophy was studied as much by Arabs as by Jews.

Several Hispano-Hebrews found favour with certain kings and occupied important posts in their courts. Those Jews in high positions acted as patrons, in the same way Hasdai ibn Shaprut had done during the caliphate. They attracted scholars, artists and poets to their courts in the same way as Moslems in equivalent positions; most poets of the time were also poets to the court.

IMPORTANT FIGURES FROM CORDOBA

We shall include those Hispano-Hebrews who were outstanding in the literary field during this period and are related to Cordoba, either by birth or from having spent a large part of their life in this city.

Among the outstanding figures of this generation perhaps the one who attracts most attention is Samuel ibn Nagrella, as he excelled as much in literary as in military and political fields. He was born in Cordoba in 993 and died in Granada in 1056. He was vizier to the Granada Kings Habbus abd Badis and conducted their military campaigns against

58

neighbouring enemy states. What has been conserved of his scientific production is a witness of his multiple talents. He carried out ample studies on the Talmud, grammar and Biblical exegesis. On the other hand he was a magnificent poet, writing poems covering the whole range of secular poetry: panegyric, poems of friendship, laments on the separation from a loved one, elegies on deaths, songs of love, bacchanal, satire, epigrams etc.

He is practically the only Hispano-Hebrew poet who composed epic poems and among his compositions we can find examples of these, describing the military campaigns he participated in. Together with these epic poems which tend to have a triumphant air as they reflect his conquests, we can also observe poems full of wisdom which reflect an existential philosophy. We find ourselves, in this case, face to face with a poet full of contrasts who brings to mind some of the principal figures in Italian Renaissance, several centuries later than the period we are dealing with.

Another great poet of this generation is Isaac ibn Gayyat (1038-1089). He was born and lived in Lucena but by pure chance he died in Cordoba, although he was buried in his native city. He presided the extremely important rabbinical academy in Lucena and disciples of his would become such famous figures as Moses ibn Ezra, Joseph ibn Sahal and Joseph ibn Saddiq. Ibn Gayyat was a close friend of Samuel ibn Nagrella and of his son Joseph, and when Samuel was murdered in Granada he took Joseph under his wing in Lucena. As an expert authority in religion, he dedicated special attention to composing sacred poetry and both Moses ibn Ezra and Al-Harizi praised his work.

In the field of grammar, two figures of this time shone with particular brilliance, both connected with Cordoba:

- *Judah ben David Hayyuy* was born in Fez towards the end of the tenth century but spent the greater part of his life in Cordoba. The period of maximum creativity in medieval Hebrew linguistics and the scientific and systematic basis for Hebrew studies were both initiated by Hayyuy. He wrote his grammar treaties in Arab, and they were later translated into Hebrew, so obtaining ample distribution among Jews living in other European countries. It is difficult to speak too highly of the importance of his work. Together with Ybn Hanah, his disciple, he reflects the highest moment of medieval Hebrew grammar.

- *Jonah ibn Yanah* was born in Cordoba and studied in Lucena. Because of the disturbances in 1012 he had to leave the city and he finally settled in Zaragoza. Many of his grammatical points of view and his lexical explanations are still valid today. With Ibn Yanah the creative stage of medieval Hebrew grammar reached its peak. From this moment on, the majority of linguists would do little other than repeat and populariza his ideas and those of Hayyuy.

Among the philosophical writers we must make special mention of Joseph ibn Saddiq (1080-1149), who was born in Cordoba and was *dayyan* (judge) in this same city from 1138 until his death. He also composed poetry and exchanged poems with his friend and great poet Judah Levi, and at the same time he was in touch with Moses ibn Ezra. He wrote liturgical poetry which was highly praised by Al-Harizi but Ibn Saddiq was above all an outstanding philosopher. His most important work was *Olam Qatam* (Microcosm); the original in Arab has not survived but we do have a Hebrew translation. Microcosm is man whose body and soul is like an imitation of the outer world or macrocosm. If man knows himself he can come to know the world and its creator - his theories stem from this starting point.

As the culmination to this chapter, we must mention, although only in passing as he will be studied in detail further on, the Hispano-Hebrew from Cordoba of greatest fame and importance; scientist, expert rabbinical authority, philosopher and doctor, Moses ben Maimon (1135-1204), better known as Maimonides.

View of Cordoba's Mosque. Door.

View of Cordoba's Mosque. Interior.

Chapter III

HASDAI IBN SHAPRUT
IN THE COURT OF ABD-AR-RAHMAN III

by JESUS PELAEZ DEL ROSAL*

I. INTRODUCTION

The aim of this chapter is to describe Hasdai ibn Shaprut's personality and to underline the important role he played not only in the court of Abd-ar-Rahman III, but also in the cultural development of the Jews in Al-Andalus. Hasdai was the instigator behind what has been called "literary and scientific renaissance of Spanish Jews" in the times of the Cordoba caliphate.

However, as we are going to talk about Al-Andalus and the caliphate, it seems a convenient moment to make a few simple and perhaps unnecessary references to the geographical extension of Al-Andalus, its different ethnical groups and the political activity carried out by Abd-ar-Rahman III.

*Commissioner to the 850th Anniversary of the birth of Maimonides (1985) and Professor of Philology. Cordoba University.

1. AL-ANDALUS AND ANDALUSIA

In order to fully understand the importance of the Cordoba caliphate, it is essential to remember that Al-Andalus did not correspond geographically in those times with what is today Andalusia. The name Al-Andalus appeared for the first time as synonymous to Spania on an Arab coin, a bilingual dinar, from the year 716. Al-Andalus was never Andalusia with the boundaries we know today: it had a much greater extension from the 8th. to the 13th. century, and smallest from the 13th. to the end of the 15th. In the times of the Cordoba caliphate, Al-Andalus covered the greater part of what are today Spain and Portugal.

The most important political and cultural centre in Al-Andalus, or Moslem Spain, was Cordoba, the capital of the caliphate.

2. THE POPULATION IN AL-ANDALUS

The population in Al-Andalus was made up of different ethnical groups: Arabs, Berbers, natives -Muladies (Spanish converts to Islam) or Mozarabs (Christians who lived among the Moors in Spain)- slaves importe from Europe, and Jews.

However, the greater part of the population was made up of natives with no difference between the Visigoths and Suebi, conquerors of the 5th century and the Iberian Romans who had merged with them. A large part of this native population converted to Islam, giving rise to *Muladies* (from the Arab *muwallad* = adopted), very often born of mixed marriages and who, in the 10th. century, were no longer distinguished from Moslems of pure Arab origin.

But not all the natives were converted to Islam; those who continued being Christians soon adopted the Arab language and culture and were known as Mozarabs.

Finally, and also forming part of Moslem Spain, were the Jews who, badly treated by the Visigoth rulers, had welcomed the Arab invaders with open arms. An important part of the benevolent attitude of the Arabs towards the Jews was due to the affinity of race and language between both groups, and this fact was to contribute towards the improvement of social conditions for Spanish Jews under the tolerant Arab dominion. Thanks to this tolerance, some centres where almost the entire population was Jewish prospered rapidly in Al-Andalus, like Lucena in the Cordoba province. In a *Responsum* from R. Notrani, gaon in Sura (853) it is stated that Lucena was *a city with many Jews....hardly a gentile among you.* Cities with a dense Jewish population were also Granada and Tarragona which Arab geographers in the 13th. century referred to as "Jewish cities". Cordoba had one of the most important Jewish communities in the caliphate period.

3. ABD-AR-RAHMAN III

Abd-ar-Rahman III (912-961) managed to pacify Moslem Spain. After subjecting dissident political powers, he restores a united and powerful kingdom, and its high cultural level enjoyed a great reputation throughout Europe. According to the *Cronica anonima* and other documents, Abd-ar-Rahman adopted the title of Caliph in 929, as well as the honorific title of *al-Nasir li-din Allah* (one who fights victoriously for Allah's religion), one year after subduing Ibn Hafsun's rebellion and having obtained the first victories over the Christian states.

Caliph Abd-ar-Rahman III maintained an intelligent policy of religious tolerance, overcoming tribal barriers and reinforcing the central authority. His success was not only due to his military power, but mainly to his political ability. He conceived the idea of conciliating the followers of different religions and the members of different ethnical groups who lived under him, turning them into a nation. As a consequence, a period of economic prosperity, peace and religious tolerance was inaugurated.

This is the geopolitical and social framework in which an outstanding figure was to appear: Hasdai ibn Shaprut, a Jew in the court of Abd-ar-Rahman III.

II. HASDAI IBN SHAPRUT.
PORTRAIT OF AN OUTSTANDING FIGURE

1. CHILDHOOD AND ADOLESCENCE

According to what Moses ibn Ezra says in his book *Kitab-al-Mudahara wa-l-Mudakara* (Book of discourse and record), Hasdai, whose full name was Abu Yusuf Hasdai ben Ishaq ibn Shaprut, was born in Jaen. His father, Isaac ben Ezra ibn Shaprut, was a rich and pious man, devoted in body and soul to the Jewish faith. Among other activities he had founded a synagogue in his native city, Jaen, and patronized scholars who studied the Torah and writers who dedicated their lives to literature.

Hasdai ibn Shaprut was born about 910. As from a very early age he was initiated by competent teachers in the study of the Sacred Scriptures and in other traditional Jewish subjects, although to tell the truth, he had no particular vocation towards these matters. As a youngster he was keen on studying languages and learnt both written and spoken Arab very well; he studied Latin with Christian teachers, members of the Mozarab clergy in Cordoba and, like the majority of Andalusians of his time, was familiar with the Romance language.

But the most fervent desire of this young Jew was to study medicine to which he dedicated himself full time and with great enthusiasm, using books written by Arab doctors in the Near East containing the basic principles of Greek medical knowledge.

Hasdai ibn Shaprut was also notable for his character; he knew how to treat people so as to gain their confidence, he possessed a brilliant intelligence and confidence both in himself and in his future.

While his companions and friends married, he remained single in spite of a letter sent to him in which the desire was expressed that he find *a dear and graceful wife adapted to him, who would help him and give him children and grand-children who would dedicate themselves to what is more precious than pearls* (the study of the Torah).

2. HASDAI, PHARMACOLOGIST

It would not take long for Hasdai to obtain scientific prestige. A discovery in the pharmacological field would make him specially famous: he rediscovered theriaca, a kind of penicillin in those days, medicine of ample use valid for curing different illnesses and used specially as an antidote for poisonous animal bites.

Theriaca had been known of since the 1st. century B.C. when it was discovered by King Mythridates Eupator; later, Andromaque of Crete, doctor to the Emperor Nero, had perfected it, creating a drug composed of 61 elements. This pharmacological product was known throughout the whole world. In the 2nd. century A.D. it was commonly produced in the Roman Empire, but its formula had gone astray and nobody had been able to find it. Among the components of this medicine Medieval doctors mention opium, roast lizard's meat and different spices.

Hasdai, after arduous investigation, at last hit on the formula and this discovery enabled him to form part of the group of physicians in the court of Abd-ar-Rahman III. Hasdai was then about thirty years old.

But things did not stop there, it was just the beginning of a rising career to power. Abd-ar-Rahman soon discovered how gifted his young physician and doctor was, and, in view of his qualities, made him *head of customs,* an important post in the caliphate administration with the task of collecting duties from boats that arrived in and departed from Spain. He dealt with economical sums which, according to a letter to the king of the Khazars, totalled a hundred thousand dinars in today's money, perhaps the most important part of the state's income. In this same document Hasdai expresses himself in these terms: *...through me* (foreign kings and grandees) *offer their gifts* (to the Cordoba monarch); this leads us to suppose that he held a post in the Caliph's palace similar to that of *head of public relations* or ambassador's go-between.

Nevertheless, despite young Hasdai's qualities, the Caliph did not make him minister of state finances *(khazin),* maybe so as not to provoke the Moslems' wrath; the appointment of non-Moslems to occupy important administrative posts always came up against opposition on the part of the Islam people, who did not look kindly on members of other creeds occupying such high positions, and not just through jealousy or envy, but also because they despised anyone who did not respect Mohammed, convinced as they were of the superiority of Islam over other creeds.

Hasdai himself was the object of envy on the part of Moslems. Averroes (1126-1198) refers in his Poetica to a faqi who wanted to provoke a confrontation between Abd-ar-Rahman and Hasdai, accusing Abd-ar-Rahman in these terms: *The prophet, who you fail to honour because of him, is said by him* (Hasdai) *to be a liar.*

The arrival of Hasdai at Abd-ar-Rahman's court, as doctor and head of customs, meant that through his meetings with the Caliph the latter came to know and appreciate him more and more. His knowledge of languages, especially Latin, the language used by the Christian states from the north of Spain in their negotiations with the Caliph, would be extremely useful and Abd-ar-Rahman was to make use of Hasdai's services as translator and interpreter in matters which required the knowledge of this language.

We must emphasize in this context the role of Hasdai in the translation of Pedanios Dioscorides' treatise *De Materia Medica,* a present to the Caliph from Constantine VII. This was the story: Constantine VII, Emperor of Byzantium (945-959), who was aware of the antagonism that existed between the Spanish monarchs and the Fatimid caliphs in Egypt and who, on the other hand, was suffering the effects of the latter's expansion, got in touch with Abd-ar-Rahman in 947 to sign a treaty of friendship, sending a eunuch to Cordoba. The Caliph, who was also interested in obtaining the King of Byzantium's support in view of the Fatimid threat, agreed to the emperor's request and sent a delegation to Constantinople in 949, presided by Hisham ben Kulaib, a Christian priest. In the spring of 949 another Byzantian delegation left Constantinople and arrived in Cordoba on the ninth of September in the same year, to be welcomed by Abd-ar-Rahman with all kinds of honours. At the head of the delegation was Stephanos, head of protocol at the emperor's court. We know very little of what was said in the messages transmitted orally by the emperor's emissaries to the caliph, and of Hasdai's role on this occasion or of the subjects discussed by the emissaries and the caliph, as Arab historians hardly say anything at all. One of them mentions the signing of a treaty of friendship and collaboration between the emperor and the caliph as a result of this meeting.

However, we do have full details of the gifts presented by the Byzantine emperor's emissaries to the caliph. Ibn Gugul describes the scene:

"He (Abd-ar-Rahman) received from Romanus, Emperor of Constantinople - in the year 337/948 I believe - a letter accompanying gifts of great value; among them was Dioscorides' treatise, illustrated with magnificent Greek miniatures and written in Greek, which is the same language as Ionian, and a book of Orosius' Historia on earlier events, former kings and important facts. The emperor wrote in his letter to Al-Nasir: "You will only be able to benefit from Dioscorides through a translator accustomed to Greek and familiar with the properties of these drugs. If you should find in your country a person who possesses both conditions, this book will be of maximum utility to you. As far as Orosius' book is concerned, you have in your Latin states persons who can read it in the original and if you hand it to them, they will translate it into Arab".

Ibn Gugul adds:

"Among the Christians in Cordoba there was no-one capable of reading Greek, which is ancient Ionian. So the Dioscorides' work lay in Abd-ar-Rahman al Nasir's library awaiting an Arab translation: it was in Al-Andalus, but the inhabitants used a translation from Baghdad, by Stephanus. When Al-Nasir replied to Romanus, he asked him to send him someone who spoke both Greek and Latin who would teach these languages to his slaves and the latter could in this way become translators. Emperor Romanus sent him a monk called Nicholas, who arrived in Cordoba in 340/951. At that time there were several doctors in the city who were investigating. researching and trying desperately to find a way of dis- covering the names of the simples in Dioscorides - the Arab equivalents were as yet unknown. The most interested and diligent of the doctors was the Jew Hasdai ben Basrut, who was eager to please Abd-ar-Rahman in this. Nicholas, the monk, became his most intimate and appreciated collaborator. In this way he was able to expound the names of the simples in Dioscorides work which were still unknown".

A few explanations will lead to a better understanding of the text quoted:

- Dioscorides' book was a collection of all the discoveries in the pharmaceutical field in Greece, enriched by a description of about 600 medicinal plants, oils and minerals. An Arab version of this book, translated by the Greek monk Stephanos, was in circulation, but this translation was far from being perfect as the greater part of the unidentified plants had not been translated. These names were written in an Arab transcription of Greek and Ibn Gugul called them "simples".

- Ibn Gugul confuses in the text the name of the emperor, calling him Romanus instead of Constantine and he refers to Hasdai ibn Shaprut as Hasdai ibn Basrut.

- Hasdai was able to translate all the names into Arab, thanks to his knowledge of Latin; it was in this language that he conversed with Nicholas the monk, who spoke both Greek and Latin.

But Hasdai was not just a translator, he was also a clever *interpreter and diplomat*. The Caliph had to request his diplomatic intervention on two occasions at least:

- Otto I (936-973), Emperor of the Sacred Roman Empire, decided to finish with a series of uncontrolled groups of Spanish Saracens who were pillaging along the coasts of France and Italy, creating an atmosphere of insecurity in these regions, which were under his protection. So he sent a delegation to Cordoba in order to come to an agreement with the caliph and put an end to this vandalism. We have no trace of the message sent by way of this delegation. What is certain is that the caliph took offence on receiving it and for this reason in turn sent a delegation to the emperor with a letter full of insults to Christianism. Otto I answered by holding the Cordoba delegation for several years and sending another ambassador to Cordoba with insults against Mohammed. The context of the letter to the caliph filtered through to Cordoba before the arrival of the emissaries. Being aware Abd-ar-Rahman that the end of the emissaries would be the death penalty - as the Koran decrees death not only for anyone who offends Mohammed, but also for the person who should apply this penalty and fails to do so - and not wanting to fall out with the emperor, Abd-ar-Rahman decided to entrust Hasdai with the difficult diploma- tic task of finding out the exact content of the filtered message, and of convincing the emissaries not to hand it over. Hasdai, not without great difficulty, managed to do this, once we had won the friendship of the Abbot who led the delegation, Johannes of Gorze. In the end, the emperor was consulted once more and the Abbot only presented the gifts he had brought, trying to reach an agreement that would bring an end to the incursions on the part of the uncon- trolled Saracen groups. This was in the year 956.

Hasdai was the protagonist of another important diplomatic mission:

Sancho I, King of Leon, was very fat. His obesity apparently prevented him from riding a horse and he even needed to lean on someone to walk. For this reason he had become the object of ridicule, also being accused of having lost his mind because of his excessive weight, and his rivals, the nobles in Leon, decided to depose this ridiculous and disabled king. Fernán González - who was eager to be proclaimed creator of kings and had already attempted unsuccessfully on one occasion to put a king on the throne - encouraged unrest among the subjects in Leon. A conspiracy was hatched in the army and one spring day in 958 the King found himself without a kingdom. Sancho I fled to Pamplona, to his grandmother, Queen Toda of Navarra. Meanwhile Fernán González and the other grandees met to choose another king. The choice fell on Ordoño IV, a cousin of Sancho's, described by historians as hunch-backed, despicable and perverted, to such an extent that from now on he would be known as Ordoño el Malo (the Bad). He was chosen as king for one single reason:he was the only adult in the royal family.

From the very first moment of the election, the old, ambitious Queen Toda of Navarra was determined to restore her grandson to the throne. In order to do this she had to find a powerful ally in military circles and, at the same time, a doctor who could cure her grandson's obesity. All this was to be found in Cordoba, a city where she would undoubtedly come across a doctor and obtain the caliph's military support. It cost the Queen a great effort to take this step as she had to ask for help from the caliph - her grandnephew - who she had been at war with for more than thirty years, and who had devastated her valleys and set fire to her cities hardly a year before. Perhaps the love of her grandson and the longing to see him back on his throne made her take the decision.

When the scheme was proposed to the caliph by means of an ambassador, he decided to send Hasdai to Pamplona. Once there, Hasdai advised the Queen cleverly, telling her it would be convenient to treat her grandson in Cordoba, where he disposed of the means for the treatment, and that the caliph, on the other hand, was prepared to send his troops to Leon but it would be better for her to travel to Cordoba and celebrate a meeting with him. He convinced them to travel to the capital of Al-Andalus, so satisfying Abd-ar-Rahman's pride and affording his people the unprecedented spectacle of a Christian Queen and two Christian Kings, the Queen's son and Sancho I, coming humbly to throw themselves at his feet to beg his support. In the negotiations, Hasdai managed to obtain the concession of ten fortresses in exchange for the promise of caliphal help. The event was celebrated with fiery verses by the two poets under Hasdai's patronage - Dunash ben Labrat and Menahem ben Saruq. This is the song the former sang:

> *Compose a song of praise*
> *In honour of our Prince, head of the Academy*
> *Who totally destroyed the foreign forces,*
> *He is girded with glory and majesty*
> *Invested with divine assistance,*
> *He snatched ten fortresses from the insolents*
> *And wrought havoc*
> *Among the thorns and thistles.*
> *He brought Ramiro's son,*
> *Princes and priests.*
> *Lord, knight and king*
> *He brought like a pawn*
> *Sceptre in hand*
> *To an enemy people;*
> *He also dragged the simple,*
> *Ancient Toda,*

Who wore her royalty
Just like a man,
With the strength of his wisdom
With the power of his astuteness
With the multitude of his subtleties
And the sweetness of his words.

Finally, as a result of the meeting, the Moorish armies together with those of Navarra attacked Leon and Castile in 959; a year later, Sancho I acceeded once more to his throne, cured of his obesity. Fundamentally, the cure consisted of certain herbs and of physical exercise. Apparently, on Hasdai's advice, Sancho I marched on foot all the way from Pamplona to Cordoba.

5. HASDAI, PRINCE OF THE JEWISH COMMUNITIES IN AL-ANDALUS

In spite of his privileged position in Abd-ar-Rahman's court, Hasdai never forgot his origin nor his Jewish con- dition . From his powerful position he would make the most of every opportunity to help his people.

Abd-ar-Rahman, in view of Hasdai's Jewish condition, named him *nasi* or Prince of the Jewish communities in Al-Andalus. The Jews, however, considered the election of Hasdai for this post not so much a recognition of his ability or wisdom as a direct intervention of divine pro- vidence protecting the Jews. We do not know exactly what the attributions or duties were of the Andalusian nasi, as no document referring to them has been conserved. But there is no room for doubt that he must have been the maximum legal power within the Jewish community, with coercive force, and in any case being his obligation to seek the well-being of his people.

As *nasi*, comments J.M. Millas Vallicrosa, Hasdai was delegated with jurisprudence over all the Jewish communities within the caliphal dominions; he maintained relations with Talmudical academies in Iraq, especially with those of Sura and Pumbedita; on the other hand, he was in touch with the

Hebrew schools, very flourishing at that time, in Kairuan and Constantine and received scientific tracts from all of them. In particular we know of an astronomical tract that he received about the celestial orb, determining the course of the stars, using an appropriate instrument, that is, the alcora.

Hasdai's relations with the Jewish communities were not limited, as we have said, only to the communities in Al-Andalus. They spread much further than the frontiers and reached the far corners of the earth. His intentions in this sense were ambitious: he wanted to obtain as much information as possible from all the Jewish communities in the diaspora; he always intervened in favour of persecuted or oppressed communities and carried out a cultural patronage in three directions: he gave financial support to the rabbinical schools, entrusted them with the editing of books on subjects of interest and imported books from libraries or cultural centres in the East. All this is reflected in a letter to the King of the Khazars which reads:....*I never fail to ask all ambassadors who bring gifts if they have news of our brothers, those of them saved from exile, in case they have heard something of the liberation of the rest, consumed by labour without having found repose.* This letter offers valuable information about Abd-ar-Rahman and Al-Andalus or Sefarad, its extension, economic and cultural relevance, the army, Court revenue and international relations. It was sent to the King of the Khazars to find out as much as possible about this Jewish kingdom, where the governors and the majority of the people were Jewish, situated on both banks of the Lower Volga, between the Caspian and Crimean seas, and about the Caucasus to the south, made up of peoples of Turkish origin, converted to Judaism towards the middle of the 8th. century. This kingdom seems to have disappeared in the second half of the 10th. century or first half of the 11th.

We also have news of the contacts Hasdai maintained with the *Jews in the south* of Italy from a letter they sent him. In it they apologize for the delay in answering Hasdai's letter because of the persecution they were suffering. In this letter they enclose a list of the rabbis and Torah scholars who had survived and at the same time inform him of the development and circumstances of the persecution.

73

The persecution referred to in the letter is undoubtedly the one provoked by a decree proclaimed against the Jews by the Byzantine emperor Romanus I Lekapenos, who ruled from 919 to 944 and persecuted the Jews, obliging them to convert to Christianism or condemning them to exile. The same letter relates how two scribes, Rabbi Isaiah and Rabbi Menahem, with their disciples Rabbi Elijah preferred to commit suicide rather than suffer forced conversion to Christianism. Although the authors do not ask Hasdai for help in this letter, he did not hesitate to come to their aid, inter- ceding before the Byzantine emperor. When, in 948, Abd-ar-Rahman sent an ambassador to the emperor, Hasdai had the delegates take two letters written in Hebrew to the Royal Court at Constantinople. Hasdai's appeal on behalf of the Jews in Italy found favour with the emperor and so as to avoid complications he agreed to the condition that the intervention was not effected in his name but in that of Hasdai; the emperor did not want to appear as a defender of the Jews.

The first of the two letters was sent to a noble lady, possibly the Empress Helen, daughter of the Emperor Romanus I Lekapenos. In it the Jews are referred to as *the rest of the survivors of the community among us* and begs her not to oblige them to act against their will, suggesting that she name *one of her subordinates to deal specifically with Jewish matters.* To give weight to his petition, Hasdai promised to act in favour of the Christians in Spain, something which he says he was already doing. The second letter was to Constantine VII Porphyrogenitus. It was written in diplomatic style but we know little of its content as the text has only survived in incomplete fragments.

Finally we are aware that Hasdai also intervened in favour of the Jews in the south of France, a subject state of the great Germanic kingdom. In the city of Toulouse existed the following custom: on the eve of the Passover a Jew had to present himself at the cathedral door and offer thirty pounds of wax for the lighting of candles in the Church. The Bishop stood by the door and when the Jew presented his offering, the Bishop slapped his face. This took place every year. On one occasion the Bishop hit the Jew so hard that he died. This was the way the Christians in that city commemorated the gospel story of the thirty silver coins that Judas Iscariot betrayed Jesus for. The letter from Hasdai was sent by way of Samuel, a member of the caliph's embassy, to King Otto I and delivered on his way through Toulouse. In this case, Hasdai's appeal does not seem to have had much result as the custom continued for another hundred and fifty years after the letter was sent.

The fame of Hasdai's protection of the Jews made many of them immigrate to Moslem Spain in Abd-ar-Rahman's time, especially from Morocco, as the Fatimid military campaigns and Berber pillaging created an atmosphere of terror that made many Jews in this country cross the Strait in search of peace and quiet in Al-Andalus. Most of them came from Fez, where there was an important Jewish community.

6. HASDAI, CULTURAL PATRON

We cannot complete this portrait of Hasdai without drawing special attention to his activity as patron of poets and philologists. His activity in this field was immense and the poet Dunash ben Labrat sings:

> Clouds are his hands
> For the poets:
> In winter they rain
> And in summer shower
> Gold and jewels ,
> Onyx and precious stones.
> For the sons of Torah
> He is salvation and light.
> His riches come to Sura
> In exchange for books
> To instruct them in the precepts
> That are sweet as honey...

There are numerous testimonies that speak of his work as a promoter of culture in this period; we have chosen one, perhaps the most eloquent, a fragment from Al-Harizi's book *Tahkemoni*:

All the wise men of his generation gathered round him (Hasdai), shining like brilliant lights, to pass on their wisdom to all who seek God. He filled them with God's spirit, with wisdom and intelligence, with prodigal knowledge, with the art of shaping ideas and kindling fire in their hearts. From that time on, sciences opened a breach in Spain, the headstrong learned doctrine, followed by the poets. His generosity made the tongues of the dumb sing forth and closed hearts opened up to compose delightful poems that shone like the stars on high. Then their eyes beheld poetic art, the skies opened wide and divine visions appeared. In his times wisdom spread throughout Israel, for he was the redeemer and supporter of science. After those times the light of brilliant minds went out.

In conclusion we must emphasize Hasdai's efforts as what we could be called *the founder of the school for Hebrew Philology in Cordoba*. With this object in mind he had Menahem ben Saruq come from Tortosa and, promising to pay all his costs, entrusted him with certain research into the language which could be none other than the confection of the Hebrew dictionary, the Mahberet. Menahem became director in Cordoba of a school of Hebrew philological studies centered around the investigation of the Hebrew language and Bible interpretation.

We do not know exactly why, but Hasdai's behaviour towards Menahem left a lot to be desired, as he did not keep his promise to pay his keep and when he did so, Menahem, out of pride, rejected the ridiculous sum Hasdai wanted to pay him. Menahem fell so much into disgrace that Hasdai ordered his house to be demolished and confiscated all his belongings, sending him to prison and later expelling him.

This fact, after such an amount of brilliant activity that we have described, provides a human counterpoint to the great figure of Hasdai, who, like all human beings, also had a darker side. The positive testimonies in praise of this personality whose portrait we have drawn, have passed into History; the poems that speak of him are for the most part, if not actually paid for, at least composed in order to obtain benevolence from the all powerful Hasdai, a Jew, originally from Jaen and settled in Cordoba, in the Court of Abd-ar-Rahman III.

Chapter IV

JEWISH POETS IN CORDOBA

by ANGEL SAENZ BADILLOS*

I believe there is no other city in the world that Hebrew poetry owes so much to, as to Cordoba. Cordoba is the home of Hispano Hebrew poetry, the laboratory where the most fundamental changes in technique and subjects were initiated and materialized. The results, of course, spread beyond the limits of the city, reaching many other places in the peninsula. But Cordoba can always take pride in the fact that it was here the first important examples of Hebrew Spanish poetry were written, that here a large number of the most famous Spanish Jewish poets were born, and lived or spent part of their life.

The Hispano Hebrew poetry that began to develop in the Cordoba caliphate half way through the 10th. century is the result of the union of very diverse traditions and elements, merging in a new and original way which would soon give fruits of the highest poetic quality. On the one hand, the tradition peculiar to the Jewish people, the first biblical examples of which go back to the end of the second millennium B.C. Almost without a solution of continuity, the Palestine Jews have carried on their poetical activity for hundreds of years, improving their technique little by little, introducing

*Profesor of Hebrew Language and Literature. Granada University

rhyme... Apart from rare exceptions, this poetry has always enjoyed a regular place in the Synagogue, accompanying and enriching the Jewish people's prayers.

This abundant vein, nourished by language and traditions from the Bible, would be enriched precisely in Cordoba by another completely different poetical tradition: that of the Arab poets, who had also been singing praises. laments, to love and beauty in the language of the Koran for many hundreds of years. The Jewish poets in this city were able to appreciate the beauty of Arab poetry and would begin to emulate it using the language of the Scriptures. And not many years would pass before they would also assimilate the rhythm of popular tunes, in Romance, that common people sang; a rhythm they would also attempt to reflect and imitate in their *muwashshahat*, very often terminating with those unequalled stanzas in Romance - the *Khardjas*. In this way, three different cultures would merge successfully in one single language and I feel I am not exaggerating when I say that it is above all in Cordoba where this multiple birth takes place.

1. HASDAI, PROTECTOR OF POETS

Under the shadow of the tolerant Abd-ar-Rahman III, a Jew, native of Jaen, Hasdai ibn Shaprut was able to hold important posts in the Court, and carry out an ample activity there, not only in the field of medicine (his speciality) but also in diplomatic and political fields. The first Jewish poets we know of in Spain would find help and protection in his house. As secretary, he took on Menahem ben Saruq from Tortosa, who wrote some of his important letters to far off illustrious personalities. And another of his protegees, Dunash ben Labrat, would write of Hasdai:

His hands are clouds,
For the poets,
In winter they rain
And in summer shower.

that is to say, his generosity flows over the poets in abundance. Some of the first poems conserved of this time are precisely panegyrical, dedicated to the praise of this famous Cordoba courtesan. So his figure is closely connected to the first poetical steps in this city. It is the first time in the history of the Jewish people that we have news of this type of "family poet" such as this case in Ibn Shaprut's house in Cordoba; this poet cum secretary found in the person of his patron a way of earning his living which would enable him to carry out poetical and philological activities. Hasdai created the appropriate atmosphere for promoting letters and philology. In their long peregrination through strange countries, the Jews had never before found such a favourable atmosphere to set their creativity free.

2. MENAHEM BEN SARUQ, POET AND PHILOLOGIST

Halfway through the tenth century the post of family poet cum secretary to the Ibn Shapruts was occupied by this Jew from Tortosa who would obtain the merit of compiling the first dictionary of biblical roots in Hebrew, a work as yet rudimentary but of great value and interest, undertaken as a result of a commission on the part of his patron. When necessary, wrote poems of circumstance, for example, on the death of Hasdai's mother. Few of his works of art have survived; one of the most important is the letter from Hasdai to the King of the Khazars, a distant state that seems to have converted to Judaism and in which the occidental Jews appear to have seen a flash of Messianic expectation. The letter, in verse, shows the secretary's signature, Menahem ben Saruq, in the first letters of some lines. Technically speaking, it shows no innovations, but the subject is unusual in Jewish poetical tradition; it is a panegyric to the King and all his people, its language is full of biblical sentences and allusions:

A crown is the apparel of the dominant tribe, the far

kingdom.
The favour of God be with him and His peace with all the chiefs and numerous army.

His aid covers His territory , His congregation and His assembly like a veil.
The strength of His hosts and His warrior chiefs take refuge in his wonderful Hand.

The horses of His carriages and His riders never retreat with humbled spirit;
His captains' standards and His soldiers' bows are covered in glory;
His archers' arrows and the brilliance of His lances strike through the heavy smoke,
Piercing the hearts of my Lord King's enemies to complete their destruction.

In His horses' necks there is strength, excitement and threat;
His riders victorious, come return safe and sound from the terrible country.

So my soul proclaims: Happy the eyes that behold our King coming out on the battle day,
Like a bright and admirable sun;

His soldiers speed like thunderbolts - two are worth ten thousand, one like a hundred,
They crush their enemies like an overloaded cart collapsing.

Take heed, columns of the earth: who has ever seen such a thing,
That a fugitive dominate the mighty who flee giving up the city and all within it?

The arm of Elyon is their strength and aid, and causes terror;
That is what Sadday does, punishing the transgressing kingdom as it deserves;

*Multiplying the splendour and lordly beauty of the nation
he carries from the womb.*

*I remember the ancient prodigies, the great rage and
terror of affliction;
When it lay back limp, upon its excrement,
Only its distinction remained, and there it is, dispersed to
the winds and corners.*

*Toasted by the sun that poured down relentlessly;
It has not been redeemed, the moment of liberation has not
yet come;
A hole has been bored as if it were an ear, it has not come
out into freedom;
It has been left afflicted and drunk without tasting wine;
Its ravagers have laid hands on it, obliging it to leave its
sanctuary.*

*The times and days have become long and weary, but no
sign appears;
No prophet nor prophecy remain, and neither Spirit nor
vision come forth.* ◦
*The visions of the favoured man are not revealed and no
prophecies are left.*

*Before God, who is my strength with thirsty soul I will
open my hands:
Gather those dispersed and spread about the furthest
corners of the devastated earth,
That those in anguish about the date may say: the awaited
time has come.*

*David's dwelling, the great King's city will vomit them as
before;
The eyes of those that remain will see strength set on high,
The son of Yisay's kingdom in the secret of the prophet's
vision:
"I will make your iron horn" forever, from that day on.*

This is vigorous language, splendidly describing the situation of the Jewish people in the diaspore, the expectance of liberation increased by the success obtained by its people in the far of Khazars kingdom, near the Caucasus. What is new, I must insist, is the subject matter and the form of poetic epistle found here, something almost unknown in Hebrew literature up to that moment. We also have some other panegyrical poems and other odd poetical letters by the same author, like the one written to Hasdai protesting about treatment received and injustices suffered. We have no trace of any other author who had dealt with these subjects before in Hebrew. An important step had been taken in Cordoba.

3. DUNASH BEN LABRAT

Another even more decisive step was taken by a Jew who had come from Babylon, disciple of the great gaon of oriental Judaism, gaon Saadya: Dunash ben Labrat.. Possibly his family was from Fez; he was captivated by the splendour of the Caliphate and moved to Cordoba, where he became a Sephardi by adoption. He published the most important part of his work here and had the opportunity to put his ideas into practice, ideas that combined reform and tradition. He clashed directly with Menahem: the young and cultured man familiar with the most advanced knowledge of his time opposed to the provincial Menahem, almost self-taught. The almost inquisitional tone used by Dunash is not at all to our liking. He is almost certainly largely to blame for his rival falling into disgrace. But times are not easy for Judaism, and defence in the face of sectarian and heretical spirits is something all traditional and pious Jews carried inside them. This may explain the ease with which Dunash criticizes Menahem.

Those replies to Menahem ben Saruq, Dunash's Teshubot, have a special meaning for us. The book is prefaced by a panegyric in honour of their common patron, Hasdai ben Shaprut. This panegyric is the first example we have of a poem written in Hebrew according to the requirements of quantitative metre in Arab poetry. Since the far off times of pre-Islamic tribes in the Arabian desert, the Arabs used to write their poems with play on the alternating of long and short syllables and accents in fixed places; the result was a special kind of rhythm, with rich sound effects. Nothing like this had ever been attempted in Hebrew poetry up to that moment. And Dunash dared to take the decisive step: by way of a clever adaptation he overcomes the differences that exist between the two languages (in Hebrew there is no distinction between long and short syllables), and manages to open up a totally new horizon in his people's poetry. Although at first many are reluctant, the most brilliant examples of Hispano Hebrew poetry were written in this quantitative metre adapted from the Arabs by Dunash. For it is not only this formal technique but the patterns of poetical compositions themselves, the subjects and figures, all that possesses most beauty in Arab poetry finds its way into Hebrew poetry through him, merging with language and matters from the Bible to produce a new and vigorous synthesis.

Dunash himself takes the first tentative steps in this new direction which a few years later will lead to the fulfillment of the Jewish Spanish Golden Age. But his poetry is representative at least of this synthesis of Arabic-Spanish sensualism and traditional Jewish conditions. We have here some lines from this panegyric:

Let my heart know wisdom, intelligence and right,
Keep to the prudent ways, listen to the teaching
Seek justice and do not be obstinate,
So that you may not fall into the trap like the hearts of the perverse...

Do not long for wine, long time kept
Whose aroma does not change when it settles on the sediment,
Nor drink it arrogantly in golden cups
Nor see it sparkle in sapphire goblets
Nor select victuals, all kinds of delicacies,
In the shady gardens, surrounded by streams,
Fragrant flowers and fine looking sweet fruits

And overflowing fountains, pools and waterways
Watched over by deer like those in the woods...

All this is vanity for ruin and grief;
Its merriment is mourning and its sweetness bitter;
It begins in pleasure and ends in moans,
Groans and lamentations, tumult and affliction...

And after this somewhat conventional introduction, the praise itself:

Sing a song of praise in honour of our prince, head of the
Academy,
Who totally destroyed the foreign forces.
He is girded with glory and majesty
Invested with divine assistance.
He snatched ten fortresses from the insolent
And wrought havoc
Among the thorns and thistles...

Nations take fright, peoples tremble,
The brave lose heart in their fear of him
Every king quakes and descends from his throne
And sends him gifts as far as Sepharad...

His master's political achievements, his generosity to the needy and to scholars are exalted in these "new and brave scanned verses" that he introduces into Hebrew literature.

The following example of Bacchic poetry is also representative of this moment in Hispano Hebrew poetry; the first part is the classical invitation to drink and the pleasure which usually accompanies drinking, described with all the sensuality of Arab poetry which we have referred to before. In the following generations Hispano Hebrew poets would write several similar poems which on many occasions are nothing but a form of aesthetic exercise. But Dunash, who is undoubtedly one of the first Jewish poets who ventures to touch such subjects (if not the first), adds a second part, presenting a different aspect of life, as seen by a pious Jew in the diaspore in the 10th. century; there can be no real joy in life for any Jew while his people's destiny pursues its tragic course and exiled from his country. Immersed in the tranquil and tolerant life in Cordoba, full of pleasure, the Jew is still aware of his situation as a person and as a member of a people overwhelmed by calamities:

He said: "Do not sleep! Drink old wine,
Amidst myrrh and lilies, henna and aloes,
In an orchard of pomegranates, palms and vines,
Full of pleasant plants and tamarisk;
To the hum of fountains and the throb of lutes,
To the sound of singers, flutes and lyres.

There every tree is tall, branches are fair with fruit,
And winged birds of every kind sing among the leaves.;
The doves moan melodiously,
And the turtle-doves reply, cooing like reed pipes.

There we shall drink among flower-beds fenced in by lilies,
Putting sorrow to rout with songs of praise.
We shall eat sweets as we drink by the bowlful,
We shall act like giants, drinking out of huge goblets.

And in the mornings I shall rise to slaughter
Fat choice bulls and rams and calves;
We shall anoint ourselves with fragrant oil and burn aloe incense.
Oh, before doom overtakes us, let us enjoy ourselves in peace.

But I reproached him thus: Silence! How dare you,
When the Holy House, the footstall of God is in the hands of the gentiles?

You have spoken foolishly, you have chosen sloth,
You have uttered nonsense like the mockers and fools.
You have forsaken the study of the Supreme God's law.
Even as you rejoice, jackals run wild in Sion.

Then how could we drink wine, how even raise our eyes,
When we are loathed and abhorred, and less than
nothing?"

4. THE FIRST JEWISH POETESS IN SPAIN

The latest investigations carried out by professor
Fleischer, in Jerusalem, have brought to light another
interesting matter related to the Dunash family: the first
Spanish Hebrew poem that may have been written by a
woman has a concrete attribution to Dunash's wife on the
manuscript conserved. This would be one of the rare examples
- and certainly the oldest - of a poem written by a Jewish
poetess. It is a short farewell poem, of great beauty and
sensitivity, in which the poetess, her son in her arms, watches
her husband depart, leaving Spain for what we believe to be a
short spell. It would not be taking things too far to consider
that this poem was also written in Cordoba, where they lived.

Will her beloved remember his gazelle? When he departed
she was holding their dear son in her arms.
He put the ring from his right hand on her left hand, and
she put her anklet on his arm.
While she took his veil as a keepsake, he took hers as a
memento.
He would not stay in Sepharad even if he were given half
the kingdom by his master.

The poetical technique is the same as that used by
Dunash. Some scholars do not believe it was written by his
wife but by Dunash himself, replying with another similar
poem. But it may well be that we have here the first poem
written by a Jewish poetess in Spain.

88

5. MENAHEM'S DISCIPLES AND OTHER RELIGIOUS POETS

The innovations introduced by this young man who may seem affected and somewhat pert, and who dared attack Hasdai's very secretary, contributing quite a bit to his falling into disgrace, was to provoke a reaction on the part of three of Menahem's disciples. One of them, Isaac ben Capron, is also a well known poet. They answer Dunash from Cordoba, defending their teacher and severely censoring his innovations in poetical techniques, among other things, for forcing the Hebrew language. And although we have no definite proof, it is almost certain that this reaction against the novelty was accompanied by a new technical exercise that would also find an important echo in poetry on religious subjects by Spanish Jewish poets; a syllabic system that does away with the distinction between long and short syllables and is better adapted to the Hebrew language. It is in and around Cordoba where the new syllabic technique materializes and takes hold. The following is one of the first liturgical poems written in this syllabic metre, its author, Isaac ben Capron:

I am fearful before the heaven's Creator, I find no   words, my lips are mute.
Presenting myself as insignificant and humbled I shall find favour with you like the kind elder who proceeds justly.
I await your benevolence with a firm heart, and I shall speak no more, for I am young of age.
I arise and commence, with permission of great and small.

Oh Lord, with open mouth I beg, have mercy on me.
When I lift up my voice to you, hear me, for the poor man commits himself unto You (Ps. X,14) Oh Lord, eternal rock.

Oh, full of light, from your abode do not avert your eyes, take vengeance on your enemies with your right hand, Oh God.

*They have destroyed your sanctuary and brought me
down, setting nets and traps before my feet.
Our honour has been stained, our heart is sick, for we
have no father, we have been made orphans.
We are afflicted with humiliations, they burn us at the
stake, they strike your Sanctuary with clubs and
hammers.
We are dispersed and scorned in every country, people
make puns about us and treat us like fools.
They conspire and fret, scratching my back; they gossip
about me night and day.*

*Let your joy return to me hearing my cry, Oh God, King on
Your merciful throne.*

This sensation of oppression, of diaspore, and the longing for liberation that can only come from the Lord, will
appear constantly in the poetry of the Spanish Jews, in spite of
the fact that the situation in other places left much more to be
desired than in Al-Andalus. The religious poets reflected the
feeling of their people magnificently.

Another famous poet of abundant production, Joseph ibn
Abitur, closely connected to Cordoba circles, employs a very
similar tone. He lived on Cordoba for several years and after
attempting without success to have himself elected as
religious chief of the local Jewish community, spent his final
years in the East. Let us see part of one of his laments on the
persecutions suffered by his people:

*Weep my brothers and mourn for Zion with great emotion,
like Hadadrimmon (Zech XII,11) for Josiah, son of
Amon.
Weep for the tender and favoured, stepping on thistles
bare-footed, fetching water and cutting firewood for the
Ethiopians.
Weep for the one who is forced to serve without being
accustomed, who istold "load this and stand up" but he
cannot stand the load...*

90

Weep for the blind that wander about Sion, stained with blood from pregnant women cut open, with blood from the elderly and from children...
Weep for the girls liked carved columns, turned into slaves of abominable slaves.
Weep abundantly and mourn for the synagogues destroyed by the savage beast, where vultures gather.
Weep for the dispersed, assembled for the day of disgrace, and for the poor and needy, oppressed, tyrannized.
Weep much for those who live and not for the dead, for to be like them is our constant desire.
So do not console me, my friend, do not reason with me, for all those choppeddown in Sion with nobody to bury them.

6. A WANDERING BARD: ISAAC IBN KHALFUN

It is certainly not my intention to show a deformed picture of reality, to paint too black a life of the Jews in Spain during this period. The sensation of exile is but one of the multiple aspects of their life, and in caliphal Cordoba that cry referred to gives way to another, much less acute and more conventional. This is how Isaac ibn Khalfun, for example, sings:

Weep, my soul, for you have been crushed in the dust and rejected,
You are sorely grieved by the hind let loose(Gen IL,21)
Whose eyes have led your heart astray and seduced you.
With false lines she has drawn you to the fowler's snare and to the narrow
You have erred because of the flattery of her lips when she says:
"Come, beloved, come up to my spacious terrace;
There we shall take our fill of love until the morning and we shall solace ourselves.
My table is prepared for you and my heart open to you."

She will deliver the fruit of your labour into the hands of
cruel people with no qualms,
Perfumed with myrrh and with her salty censer.
And you will know and understand that that your
madness overcame you.
And do not let your soul be slashed to pieces by the sword
of justice...

And not everything would be so sad. Isaac ibn Khalfun was probably born about 970, and, though it is not certain, maybe in the very city of Cordoba. He spent at least the most important part of his life here, although he was a globe-trotter, a wandering bard trying to earn his keep under the roof of powerful people, writing what they liked to read, earning his living writing poetry. And, as we know, life has its ups and downs. Isaac make clever use of technique and touches on practically all the usual subjects of Arab poets at that moment. He enjoys life and faces up to to his destiny. There is a certain cynicism, disenchantment in his poetry. Let us see a short but significant example:

When desire arouses me, I leap like a deer to see my lady's
eyes.
But when I come, I find her mother there - and her father
and her brother and her uncle!
I look at her, then quickly turn away, as though I were not
her beloved.
I am afraid of them, and my heart mourns for her like the
heart of a woman bereft of her only son.

At times this wandering poet overcomes his sorrows and difficulties:

My calmness vanished like a cloud, while my sighs
continued,
My joy and mirth came to an end and were quenched
altogether.

The Synagogue, Cordoba. Interior.

«Judios» street in Cordoba's Jewish Quarter.

My flesh clothed in clods of dust, my bones burned with
the heat (Job VII,5; XXX,30)
My eyes without sleep, night without light,
No breath, nor strength nor calm for my troubled soul;
Like a man who sleeps at the top of the mast in the midst
of the tempest (Prov. XXIII,24).

Exile makes me role like a ball towards the city in flames.
Some days I wandered away, others afflicted and
anguished,
Without finding a resting place or bode for my footsteps.
If only Destiny had at least provided me with my keep, in
spite of everything...

And these negative experiences lead him to a very pessi-
mistic view of the world about him:

The World's face is like a leper's neck; therefore it is only
right to spit in her face.
It is fitting and proper to cast one's sandals at the nape of
her lovers and to strip them bare.
So, if you can, make them drink deep of wormwood, but
pretend to satisfy them with sweet drinks.
Then make you sword drink deep of men's blood, and do
not heed their groans.
Show no mercy to high or low but say outright:"This is
what I wish to do".
They are snakes and scorpions, these children of the
World, and even if you offer them your precious life as a
gift,
They will always betray you, as does the World herself in
time of anguish and distress.
Yes, they are just like their mother - so put them back into
her deep, wide womb,
Kill them, either secretly or in the open. God is your pledge
that you will not go down into hell.

These harsh words were directed in 1020 at the envious persons who rejoiced on seeing his friend and protector, Samuel ibn Nagrella, fall into disgrace. Although a generation separates them in age, the poetical correspondence between them which has been conserved, shows how deeply the friendship went on both sides, although their characters, ages and social positions were so very different.. Samuel ibn Nagrella, born in Cordoba in 993, spent the first twenty years of his life in this city, until the arrival of the Berbers in 1013. His political career was brilliant although he would suffer certain setbacks like the one that motivated the poem we have just seen. The relationship between both personalities was long and deep and they were to console each other on more than one occasion. Let us see another poem written by Ibn Khalfun to Samuel ibn Nagrella on the same occasion already mentioned:

Your righteousness is great and deep, your judgments are like the great mountains (Ps. XXXVI,6),
The way to righteousness, an upright heart and loving-kindness are close by you, far though they be from all men.
Great is your splendour, and those that follow your way are fed at your table without having to knock at your door.
You refuse nothing to those that beg, nor do you hold back alms from the needy.
The hearts and souls of princes pursue vanity, but your heart never forsakes mercy.
My friend, destiny has treated me badly, and has ground its teeth on me.
My lament to you is long and distended, and reaches the Lord who hears my cries.
I am anguished for you, my soul is afflicted because of your affliction.
The Lord has scrutinized and tried you with the test of the just, examining you like gold.
He has corrected you like a father corrects his only son, so that you may be wise and just.
So I rejoice, although my heart is sad, and my joy is mixed with lamentation:
When I see your sorrow, I am sad, but rejoice knowing your future is worthwhile.

94

Faithful are the wounds of a friend (Prov. XXVII,6) and
he does not chastize you to provoke your downfall;
Thus he has restored your glory according to your
faithfulness and has established your greatness as a
guide.
Take heed and be quiet (Is. VII,4), your eyes shall know
sweet sleep forever.

7. VIZIER OF GRANADA, SAMUEL IBN NAGRELLA HA-NAGID

This friend and protector of Ibn Khalfun deserves a
separate chapter. The qualities of this exceptional Jew from
Cordoba, and the success he would obtain in the Granada
Court of the Zirid Kings Habbus and Badis would convert him
into one of the most brilliant personalities of all times in
Spanish Judaism. After leaving Cordoba, Samuel would soon
reach the highest administrative posts in Granada. Between
1036 and 1056, year in which he died, he departed almost
every year, leading his master's armies into battle against
neighbouring states. At the same time he is undoubtedly his
people's spiritual leader, protecting the Jewish culture and
religion. And he is one of the most distinguished poets in the
Hebrew language, with an extensive production, of high
technical quality and profound reflection, although perhaps
excessively constrained, as he is criticized by another of his
protegees and also great poet, Solomon ibn Gabirol. Few
Hispano-Hebrew poets are as familiar with Arab culture as
with their own Jewish tradition.

Almost no other Jewish poet will leave us such poems as
his, full of life and directly reflecting reality, like those written
on the very battle field, his war poems, as cruel and bloody as
the events he describes:

The beginning of the month of 'Elul found them upon the
heads of rocks, without grass or fruit.
And we made them fall to the earth like birds who have
touched the heights and are no more.

They were scattered in four or five directions like olives shaken by a hired hand...

The wars in which he took part are really against God's enemies, and it is God himself who provides him and his armies with victory:

My friend, in times of trouble the Rock stood up in my behalf and for this I praise him,
And sing to the Lord who discerned the fear of the foe in my heart and lessened my terror.
My melodies are offered to the Healer who put balm on the hurting place and removed my pain...
How can I not compose songs to God who cured my wounds?

Samuel feels like a poet in God's Court:

Let me take sweet counsel with God in my song and he will embitter the hearts of my foes.
He is responsible for slaying my adversaries and I am beholden to entreaty him with my song.
"And to work for him like hired hand each day for He will pay my wages on time".

It is not usual for a Jew to occupy high posts at court, like Samuel does, and for this reason it is not to be wondered that he was surrounded by detractors and envy. Samuel explains their attitude with a certain fatalism which is perhaps a synthesis of Moslem and Jewish traditions:

He contends with me for my consorting with kings, I reply to him:
"This is a portion of my inheritance and my lot."
He is frightened by their rage and anger.
I answer him: "The Lord is my protection and my hope."
Whereupon he said: "What have you to do with wars?" I reply: "My death and my grave have already been determined and the Lord who informs by his seraphs in a dream, will be my help.

If I am consumed by my iniquities, - do I have a choice in the matter? all that is written in my book will (surely) come upon me!

His poetry contains many other aspects that can only be reflected here with brief examples.

Samuel knows how to combine his harsh political and military life with the light poetry popular in his time, in which he also reflects personal experiences of his life in Granada:

Behold the cold days have already passed and the season of winter's rains is buried.
The young turtle doves are seen in our land, they call to one another from the tips of branches.
Therefore, my companions, keep the covenant of friendship, make haste and do not defy me.

Come to my garden and pluck the roses whose perfume is like pure myrrh.
And by the blossoms and gathering of swallows who sing of the good times, drink ye
Wine in measures like the tears I shed over parting with friends and as red as the faces of blushing lovers.

Another important part of his work clearly carries the stamp of the sapiential books in the Bible. They are brief, profound and serious reflections on the meaning of life and human ways. Thus, these words on war:

War is at first like a beautiful girl with whom all men long to play,
But in the end like a repulsive hag whose suitors all weep and ache.

And these on human destiny:

Reflect, and you will realize how shameful is your heart's delight, which comes between two cries:
You cry when you came into the world, and others cry for you when you leave it.

Feeling of the inevitable, almost existential:

The earth is a prison to man all his life.
Therefore I say this truth to the fool:
Though you rush about, the sky surrounds you on all
sides.
Try to get out, if you can.

And with similar sentiment:

My friends, we are surrounded by a wall, and the heavens
in which there are no cracks.
We are like the yolk and white of an egg, and the world is
like an egg.
You think you can escape from this melancholy day, but
how can you flee if there is no door, nor way out?
What can we do, if God's works were first? What can we
attempt if the plan has already been fixed?

Human destiny and the mystery of death:

Man's race is directed towards the grave, like water to the
falls,
The end of all life is death, as palaces will end in ruins.
Nothing is further away from man than yesterday,
nothing nearer than the day that dawns.
But both are far off for the man imprisoned beyond the
tomb.

And, once more, the anguish of existence:

Man's stay in his mother's womb is to live in a narrow
place until the moment comes to leave it.
And the day he leaves it he enters a narrow world, to
suffer anguish from calamity to calamity.
The day he returns, he goes back to a narrow grave, to the
anguish earned through sin.
Will he always find himself pushed from one distress to
another?

What use to he who suffers are these worlds where there is no relief?

Finally, there is an aspect of Samuel that we cannot omit: he is the first Spanish Jewish poet who has left us muwashshahats, poems in verses with refrain which were composed almost certainly imitating the rhythm of popular songs in Romance that passed from mouth to mouth among the simple people of his time. Arab and Jewish poets made tasteful copies of these delightful songs that have come down to us in the khardjas, and, using them as a basis, would compose poems of greater scope. I am not saying that Samuel invented the Hebrew muwashshahats, but I do want to point out that he is the earliest poet known to have written this type of versed poems in the Hebrew language.

8. A CORDOBESE BORN IN MALAGA: SOLOMON IBN GABIROL

Although he considered himself a native of Malaga. and as such, signed several poems, the historian on Hebrew Spanish poetry, Moses ibn Ezra, would call him a few years later: "Cordobese born in Malaga and educated in Zaragoza". It is most likely that the Ibn Gabirol family was also from Cordoba, even if they had settled in Malaga. Solomon was undoubtedly one of the greatest Jewish poets in Sefarad, and I dare say one of the greatest poets ever to have written in our peninsula. We cannot but mention him here, even if we can only touch on certain aspects of his works.

Born about 1021, maturity reached him at an exceptionally early age. We have several of his poems in which he says - in that not exactly modest tone used by poets of his time - that he is only sixteen:

I am poetry, and poetry my slave. I am a harp for poets and musicians.
My poetry is like a crown for kings, tiaras on grandees' heads.

Here am I, sixteen years old, but my mind works like an eighty year old's.

His life was short, little more than thirty years it seems, and fraught with difficulties that specially affected his sensitivity. He has to find patrons, but those who appreciate him do not enjoy long lives. Let us see the brief compositions in honour of Jekuthiel, one of the people in Zaragoza who would grant him their favour and receive in return his profound friendship:

See the sun at evening time, red as though it clothed itself in scarlet;
It disrobes the north and the south, it covers the west with purple;
And the earth, now left naked, seeks refuge in the shadow of the night, and sleeps;
Then the skies darken, as if covered with sackcloth, mourning the death of Jekuthiel.

And on the same subject:

Go to those that say that time comes round and to an end:
Earth's ways are hidden from their understanding and knowledge.
You take as a guide lights that darken when their time comes.
Why do you still pay attention to their coming to an end and going out?
Ignore all that and wonder at Jekuthiel, who has fulfilled himself completely.

His personal relationship with Samuel ibn Nagrella, who appreciates and protects him, is very interesting. Ibn Gabirol has a difficult character, probably because of his physical problems, and is usually outspoken. When he states in a poem that Samuel's poetry is as cold as the snow on the Senir mountains, their friendship breaks down, hardly to be recovered later. Nevertheless, we also have beautiful poems written in honour of the vizier in Granada.

Another important aspect of his poetical creation is the formalistic line, the search for pure poetry. Nobody like Ibn Gabirol knows how to create the purest form of beauty. A composition like the following is totally aesthetical in form:

> The lip of the cup touched my lip, like the sun shines in my friend's hand. In the vine juice burns a fire that consumes me without touching my dress.
> Eyes have never seen anything like the crystal that makes a man the image of me.
> Its must speaks silently to me: "Stop, before my majesty destroys you.
> How can you compare the sun with my light, if I surpass it when I come out?
> For its body is bare, while sapphire and onyx are my vesture.
> And how can you compare my extolling effects with one that has stolen a little of my charm?"

Even more interesting is the strictly lyrical vein. In Ibn Gabirol's poetry we can see reflected the very adventure of his life, his constant searching, his thirst for wisdom and his ruthless struggle with destiny, which pursues him ceaselessly. Contrary to other Arab or Jewish poets, much more conventional, Ibn Gabirol is surely the poet with the greatest lyrical strength known in the Peninsula before the coming of the Renaissance.

Totally real and personal is this description of his search for wisdom, struggling against destiny, embodied in nature and dreams:

> I am the man who braced himself and will not desist until he fulfils his vow:
> Whose heart recoiled from his heart, whose spirit scorned to dwell in his flesh,
> Who chose wisdom even as a youth, though he be tested seven times in the crucible of Time,

Though it pull down whatever he has built, though it
uproot whatever he has planted and breach all his
barriers.
If adversity had not redoubled and the forces of destiny
closed the way, he would have reached.
The heights of wisdom and science, scrutinizing the
depths of the treasures of the mind.
But he knows that man cannot unveil mysteries until his
body has been consumed.
Yesterday I managed to obtain a little science, but destiny
rushed in to claim its price.
While I live I shall ride in search of science, although
destiny does not want to saddle its mount.
And my heart will not fail because of my fate, but will
keep its vow without breaking it.
I am fearful, my friends, of what will occur: nothing
happens to man that he has not feared.

As I slept, and the skies were spotless, the radiant pure-
hearted moon,
Led me over the paths of wisdom and, as he led me,
instructed me in his light.
And I, fearing some misfortune, was filled with pity for
his light, as a father for his first-born son.
Then the wind assailed the moon with sailing clouds, and
they covered his face with a mask.
It was as if the wind craved for streams of rain and
pressed upon the clouds to make them flow.
The skies robed themselves in darkness. It seemed as if the
moon had died, and the cloud had buried him.
And all the other clouds of heaven wept for him, as the
people of Aram wept for the son of Beor.

Then the night put on an armourplate of darkness;
thunder, with a spear of lightening pierced it;
And the lightening flew about the skies, as if it were
jousting with the night,
Spreading its wings like a bat; the ravens of the dark fled
when they saw it.
And God closed in my thoughts, he barred my heart's
desire from all sides.

*He bound my heart with ropes of darkness, yet it rose like
a warrior breaking out of a siege.*

*But I dare not hope, my friends, for the light of the moon,
which has turned into pitch-black darkness,*
*As though the clouds were jealous of my soul and
therefore deprived me of his light.*
*And when I chanced to see his face revealed, I rejoice like
a slave who sees that his master remembers him.*
*When a mortal wages war, his spear is beaten down; and
when he tries to run, his steps falter.*
*And even the man whose spirit dwells in the shining
heavens, misfortune overtakes him.*

9. OTHER JEWISH POETS IN CORDOBA

It is impossible in a few words to refer to all the Jewish
poets connected with Cordoba. We would have to speak of
Judah Levi, who came from Tudela, but during his journeys
through Al-Andalus stayed for some time in Cordoba. And the
important religious leaders of the Cordoba community at the
beginning of the 12th. century, Joseph ibn Saddiq - author of
an important philosophical work as well as his poems - and
Joseph ibn Sahl. And many other Cordoba poets that we know
very little of apart from their names: Ha-Kohen ibn al-
Mudarram, Abu Zakkariya ben Hanina, Abu Amr ibn Yaqwa
in the 11th. century, or Solomon ibn Sahl in the 12th. The list
could continue indefinitely, but this contact with the works of
the most outstanding figures will suffice for the moment.

Chapter V

CORDOBA SCHOOL OF HEBREW GRAMMARIANS

by M. ENCARNACION VARELA MORENO*

The problems that grammatical studies aroused in Al-Andalus in the 10th. century must be considered within the general situation of preocupation concerning linguistic and exegetic studies in medieval Jewish spheres, or to be more exact, within the circles in which medieval Judaism moved, as there existed a profound restlessness as far as these questions were concerned. It is evident that the deep concern on the part of the Arabs to study their language spurred cultured Jews in the south of the Iberian Peninsula into active dedication to the study of the Hebrew language.

However, this was not the only reason behind the flourishing of Hebrew grammar in Al-Andalus, and, I dare say, not even the most important. On the one hand, in cultured circles there existed authentic scientific curiosity to penetrate the mysteries of this language and even on social occasions it was fashionable among Arabs to discuss philological details and subtleties of the language. On the other hand, Jews living in Arab countries ran the risk inherent to bilinguism; remember that it was an environment in which Arab was spoken as the normal means of expression. The Jews in Moslem Spain spoke Arab, wrote poetry in Hebrew,

---

*Professor of Hebrew Language and Literature. Granada University.

philosophical tracts in Arab and, on occasions, combined both languages, like Bahya-ibn-Paquda, among others, who wrote his book *Hobot ha-lebabot* (Duties of the heart) in Arab, but with Hebrew characters.

Nevertheless, the main preocupation on the part of the Jews is not only, as in the case of the Arabs, that of speaking their language "elegantly". If they stick to bilinguism with tenacity, it is not just for aesthetical reasons, nor - although this was also important - from the desire to preserve their own identity, but particularly for the need to understand and delve into the real meaning of the Scriptures, so as to be able to keep the Law as faithfully as possible, especially at a time when *Caraism* was beginning to reappear.

The Carait sect, which began in Babylon in the 8th. century, breaking away from official Judaism and with Anan ben David as its leader, attacks the foundations of Oral Law and rabbinic tradition, advocating a return to Biblical sources, and defends a primitive sort of free examination. For this reason, the principal concern in Judaism was to discern the *meaning* of the words contained in the sacred text and so lexicography was the area that became most important within the grammatical field for the correct comprehension of Biblical and Talmudical vocabulary.

1. ORIGINS OF HEBREW LEXICOGRAPHY

The pioneers in research into the Hebrew language were not Spanish Jews; these, like the communities in the north of Africa, maintained a cultural dependence on the Babylonian Academies of great prestige in Sura and Pumbedita. Communities from other places sometimes consulted the gaons at the Babylonian school about doubts that might arise in *halakhical* matters.

Possibly, these queries made some scholars at these schools undertake the task of compounding glossaries so that the rest of the Jewish communities knew what to abide by in religious matters.

The first known author of a lexicon is Semah Gaon, who elaborated a glossary of Talmudical terms in the second half of the 9th. century. It seems that the aim was pedagogical, to facilitate the study of the Talmud. Bearing in mind that in the communities around the Mediterranean Aramaean was never a spoken language, we can assume that the purely theoretical study of this language posed the Jews in Sefarad not a few difficulties.

Semah Gaon's work, known until the 16th. century, disappeared and today we only have evidence from indirect testimonies.

The second author to undertake a similar task was the Egyptian Saadya Gaon. In his native country when he was only twenty, he composed *Egron,* a collection of Hebrew Biblical words, in order to make the poets' task somewhat easier, resolving problems of rhyme, acrostics, etc.

Saadia's explanations only consist of quoting the Biblical passage where the words appear. The idea behind this is also religious, showing .an awareness of the danger of Hebrew being forgotten by Jews who had to speak the language of the country in which they find themselves, as he says himself:

The task of studying the Hebrew language, of understand- ing and investigating it constantly is ours, of all God's people, of our sons, wives and servants so that it may never be separated from our lips. For it is the means of knowing the laws of the Torah of our Creator, which are the essence of our existence, our light and sanctuary from the very beginning and unto eternity.

Later Saadya lived in Baghdad, where he came into contact with the Arab grammatical controversies in the academies of Basora and Kufa. It appears to be during this period of his life that he began to observe the close relationship between Arab and Hebrew. In a re-edition of the *Egron* he added Arab translations for the Greek words and a third section of grammatical rules.

This step was the first stone laid by Saadya towards a *comparative* language study, and aroused deep controversy in

Jewish circles, where the meaning of the words he furnished were hotly discussed.

Another author whose work is very little known is *Abu Sahl Dunash ibn Tamim of Kairuan*. The only news we have of him is through references by Abraham ibn Ezra, who says he tried to draw a parallel between some Arab words and others from the Bible at the beginning of the 10th. century.

Also around 900, a North African from Tahort (Algiers), *Judah ibn Kores*, wrote a dictionary prompted by the fact that the Aramaean *Targum* was being forgotten and because, according to him, it was very useful to know the Aramaean translation of the Bible for an adequate understanding of Hebrew.

He does not seem to be aware of Saadya's works, although they were contemporaries, but his method is also comparative . Ibn Kores resorted to Aramaean, Arab and Berber words to compare Hebrew terms. He justifies this in his *Risala* (epistle) to the Jews in Fez:

> *"I decided to write this book so that intelligent readers realize that there are Aramaean. Arab, foreign and even Berber words mixed in the Holy language, but above all, Arab. For Arab contains many words that, if we compare them, can be seen to be Hebrew".*

He also explains his method of investigation:

> *"We begin by taking into account the Aramaean elements in the Torah then those strange words that can only be explained by the language of the Mishna and the Talmud, and finally Arab words..."*

With Ibn Kores' dictionary a solid foundation was laid for the comparative study of the Hebrew language that Saadya had initiated to a certain extent.

The fifth figure among the first to study grammar was *David ben Abraham Al-Fasi*, born in Fez, who lived in Palestine and belonged to the Carait sect. However, he was not a fanatic Carait and respected the views of Saadya and Ibn Kores, both

Radanits, and learned questions related to grammar from them.

David ben Abraham compounded a great dictionary and quotes abundant comparative Persian terms in it.

As we have said, all these authors used Arab to compare and explain Hebrew words. None of these pioneers in Grammar came from the Iberia Peninsula, but it was not unusual for cultured men and scholars from the Babylonian academies to travel to the north of Africa or to Al-Andalus, bringing with them their knowledge, not only in the Hebrew field, but also in Arab, as is the case of the Armenian Al-Kali, a cultured emigrant from Baghdad who settled in Cordoba in 942 and as a teacher acquired great prestige and popularity in this city.

2. SITUATION OF PHILOLOGICAL STUDIES IN AL-ANDALUS

While the principal centre for medieval Arab philology was to be found in the oriental academies of Basora, the Hebrew centres in Babylon and Palestine, former centres of Jewish culture, were not prominent in grammar studies. Saadya was Egyptian and other isolated figures appear in the north of Africa, but we can only really speak of a philological school years later, under the caliphate of Abd-ar-Rahman III in Cordoba. At this time Cordoba would become the Hebrew equivalent of the Arab academies in Iraq.

In 953, the gaon from Pumbedita, Aron Cohen, wrote a letter to Hasdai ibn Shaprut at the caliphal court, in which he says textually:

From remote times and up to our day wisdom has been found in Spain...
...Also on several occasions questions were sent by the Mishna in times of the wise men of learning and they provided replies. They also planted questions...

It is one of the first historical indications which appear on the Jewish intellectual activity in Al-Andalus and on the relations between wise men from the East and from the West.

In the 9th. century Talmudical circles or schools already existed. Precisely in Cordoba R. Moses Hanok founded one of these academies, according to Ibn Daud's testimony:

> *(Moses Hanok's activity) spread throughout Spain and Magreb and many disciples came to study under his guidance. All the questions that had been put (before) to the (Babylonian) academies were directed to him...(Sefer ha-Qabbalah 48.38)*

3. HEBREW PHILOLOGICAL SCHOOL IN CORDOBA. HASDAI IBN SHAPRUT

This eminent personality, doctor, born in Jaen, would play a decisive part in unifying the efforts of Spanish scholars. As well as his activity as doctor to Abd-ar-Rahman III and Al-Hakem II, we must take into account another, the principal, as *nasi* - official representative of the Jewish communities before the Caliph - once Abd-ar-Rahman's confidence had been won.

This high political post enabled him to favour his people's culture in the form of patronage. We have as a testimony of this activity a text by Al-Harizi several centuries after his death, when his activity could be seen in perspective. His Tahkemoni reads:

> *In those days a splendid sun shone in all Sepharad's firmament: the great prince R. Isaac ben Hasdai... ...All the learned men of his time gathered around him like brilliant lights, to pass on wisdom to all who seek God...*

...In his time wisdom spread throughout Israel, as he was the redeemer and supporter of science. After that time the light of those brilliant minds went out...

And indeed, Hasdai was the true founder of the Hebrew philological school in Cordoba as an official institution, under his own protection as nasi. He sent to Tortosa for Menahem ben Saruq and entrusted him with the task of compiling a dictionary - what is really known is that he was entrusted with a work - and it is assumed that this was the famous dictionary that would give rise to fierce disagree- ment among grammarians. This disagreement would be the cause of notable progress in the study of the Hebrew language.

MENAHEM BEN SARUQ

Once he had settled in Cordoba, this philologist began his lexicographical work, which he carried out with great pains under the promises and good wishes of his patron. But the relations between Menahem and his protector ran into serious problems while this work was being carried out, which gave rise to changes in circumstances, most unfortunate for Ben Saruq who found himself bereft of Hasdai's confidence and favour, and even suffered physical aggression, the confiscation of his possessions and being thrown into prison.

Let us read a letter from Menahem in which he expresses his state of mind better than any commentary:

I leave my cause in God's hands.
Tears stream from my eyes to him.
With my own mouth I beg of him,
He who succours the oppressed...
Hear my words, My Lord,
Great Prince.
You were made of earth like me.
My Maker was your Maker.
Dust is our foundation
Our days are like a shadow on the earth.

The mighty who are exalted
The same as the poor, who are humbled,
I am the humbled man,
All of them will lie down on the dust.
Though my days have not yet declined
My hour has not yet come and my days are already filled.

Menahem intimates that he has been the victim of calumny before the *nasi*. Possibly his fall is due to the accusation of Caraism which he attributes to Dunash ben Labrat. His letter continues:

They made me try the taste of death
They opened a deep pit at my feet,
They tied my ankles with ropes of wrath
They lit my belly with eternal fire...

In this way Menahem strings out a series of lamentations and provocations very close in form and content to Job's laments:

If there are words, refute and correct me again,
But with reasons, not by force!
For who will argue with one
That is stronger than him?
I will bear the ignominious punishment
I will endure deceits,
I truly know: My redeemer lives!
He will defend my cause.
He will do me justice.

Although the biography of this author is very interesting , as is the relationship with his patron, our principal objective in this case is the study of his grammatical work.

The Mahberet

Professor Nehemia Allony, researcher in Menahem's work, is the person who has made the most complete study of the disagreement that flared up between Menahem and his contemporary grammarians.

Allony has shown that in Menahem's work there are numerous indications which confirm his posture as coming very close to Caraism. Professor Saenz-Badillos, in the light of Bacher and Allony's investigations, and studying the *Mahberet* (name given to Menahem's dictionary) from the perspective of linguistic history, confirms this theory, although he considers that the unquestionable approximation to Caraism has been exaggerated.

The *Mahberet* is a lexicon of Biblical Hebrew and Aramaean written in Hebrew and classified by roots. It owes its title (leaflet) to the fact that it appeared bit by bit, like installments. Later this name was used as the title of the dictionary.

Saadya had already established that the words were made up of two elements, one fundamental (root) and the other with a subordinate function. Menahem, for the first time, classifies the words according to their fundament (root) and orders them alphabetically.

Saadya himself states in the introduction to his work that he wanted to *present the Hebrew language clearly according to the basic content of its fundaments and the essence of its roots.*

So Menahem analyses each word from a grammatical point of view and classifies diverse elements in the same group considering that they share the same root. Within each root he describes the different shades and meanings of each word, and documents them with quotations from the Bible. He also adds some grammatical explanations and, as he himself states in the introduction, attaches great importance to the meaning of each term:

113

I will begin to explain the Hebrew language, selecting each word according to its semantic content. Each word has many meanings and an intelligent man cannot understand its fundaments unless it is within the context of meaning around it in the majority of its senses...

...There are words that the context reinforces explaining them and showing us their root, and there are words that reinforce the context, explaining its interpretation and the idea behind its secret.

... There are words that the context reinforces explaining them and showing us their root, and there are words that reinforce the context, explaining its interpretation and the idea behind its secret.

Many of Menahem's linguistic ideas are indeed in the same line as Saadya Gaon's, but the fact that he only mentions him once in his work, that he differs from or dares to correct some of the great master's points, and other reasons, made them extremely suspect of Caraism in his contemporaries' eyes, especially in the case of Dunash ben Labrat, a grammarian who had come from the East and had been strongly influenced by Saadya.

Menahem's linguistic terminology

This author's linguistic terminology is very individual. In the Mahberet he takes elements from different traditional sources already used in rabbinical texts, such as *lashon* (language), *shem* (noun), *millah* (word).

From the *Masora* he takes numerous words in the phonetical field: *mappiq, milra`* etc; the names of vowels do not coincide, however, with those in the *Masora*, sometimes even calling the same vocal points by different names, which makes it difficult to identify them.

Basic terms like *yesod* or *tosephet* had already been used by Saadya.

From religious juridical language he also takes several words, like hoq (law), *din* (rule) and *mishpat* (regulation).

Faced with the necessity of expressing concepts that in theory had not yet been studied, Menahem resorts to physiological and anthropological expressions (used already in the *Sepher Yesirah)*: *'otiyyot ha-lashon* (letters formed with the tongue), *'otiyyot ha-saphah* (letters formed with the lips), *'otiyyot ha-garon* (guttural letters) etc.

Menahem has some passages of anthropomorphical tendency like the following:

"For this reason they carry *daghesh* and *raphe,* they sound strong and light according to the will (rason) of the tongue and the wish (sibyon) of the palate, the tendency *(ma'awayyim)* of the lips and the taste *(heseq)* of the mouth."

Finally, Menahem resorts to everyday language to express many of his concepts, for example: `odot (circumstances), *damah* (to be similar), *dimyon* (similar case, synonym), *garah* (happen by chance, occur) etc., etc.

In Menahem's work there is a series of extremely interesting philological details, impossible to number here. It is suffice to say that the *Mahberet* proposes a theory that, although elementary and unsystematic, is nevertheless a solid basis for later philological discussions.

DUNASH BEN LABRAT

In contrast to Menahem ben Saruq, a provincial self-taught man, Dunash represents the cultured man, educated in Saadya's Eastern school, defending traditional Jewish learning but at the same time capable of producing the greatest innovations in poetical and grammatical fields.

At an early age, Dunash had tried to apply Arab versification techniques to Hebrew metre, a task which he would later resume in greater depth. We have enough references to suppose that the great patron Hasdai asked him to come to Cordoba, and he agreed, after having spent some time in Babylon and Fez.

So, when he had settled in this Andalusian city, he became acquainted with Menahem and his work, which he reacted to by writing his *Teshubot* (Replies), a systematical criticism of nearly two hundred words that Menahem included in one root or another, ascribing them different meanings.

Dunash attacked Menahem very sharply for, according to him, *inducing simple people to error, destroying the Jewish religion and the most beautiful of languages.* His attack went so far that, as we have said before, it may have been the main cause of Menahem's falling into disgrace with Hasdai.

The Teshubot

Dunash ben Labrat's work has been amply investigated by professor Saenz-Badillos and published in a recent book with a critical edition of the Hebrew text of the Teshubot.

This work is made up of various parts. First of all, two long introductory poems, the first dedicated to Hasdai and the second to Menahem. Then follows an introduction in prose where he explains to his adversary the reasons for his antagonism. Finally comes the main part, the *teshubot* properly speaking, a series of comments respecting the terms classified by Menahem.

In this first poem Dunash expresses himself in the terms of a court poet towards his patron:

In East and West
His name is great and sublime,

Esau's house and Arabia
Come together through his benevolence.
He seeks the welfare of his people,
And rejects their enemies,
He destroys those who plot evil
And exterminates the conspirators...

In the second poem he addresses Menahem and attempts to make it clear that there is no personal animosity in his criticism:

To he who seeks knowledge
With meditation and prudence
And awakes from sleep
At dusk and dawn,
Menahem ben Saruq...
He classified the language
And discovered its secret,
Surpassing the masters
And composed a dictionary
With learning and talent...

However a few lines later he recriminates him fiercely:

He listens to corrections
With pleasure and joy...
So I want to send him my words...
It is an open refutation,
To inflame the heart
Of the one who has wrought ruin
In the souls of creatures,
Destroying their piety...

In the same way, in the introduction in prose, he exhorts him to reflect on his errors in a tone that is lenient and somewhat self-sufficient:

You must know, brother of mine, that if it were not because I love you, I would not have corrected a single word...

*God knows that if it had not been because I have observed
that your interpretation is causing harm and dissolution
in the souls of open-hearted scholars, and in many that
are considered experts, I would never have
communicated...*

Subject of consideration in Dunash' Teshubot

Dunash takes as his subject for consideration, like
Menahem, the Bible text and attempts to give a correct
interpretation for this text through the science of language.
Even bearing in mind the metaphors and similes, what he
tries to find is the direct sense of the text.

However, Dunash bases this philological exegesis on "the
fear of God", that is to say, on the traditional rules that govern
rabbinical exegesis. This author is no rationalist, but rooted in
traditional Jewish faith and attempts to reinforce that faith
with linguistic exegesis.

It was inevitable that he clash with Menahem, who
respected the text and the text only, adopting a critical
attitude towards Ibn Kores and Saadya and whose point of
view was somewhat philocaraitish for not being appreciative
enough of rabbinical tradition.

Dunash, trying always to use the tradition as a
reference, frequently resorted to the Targumin (Aramaean
translations of the Bible) and insists on the similarity between
Hebrew and Aramaean. In the same way he refers to
Masoretic tradition and challenges Menahem precisely
because he has not taken into account the Masora
recommendations.

Dunash uses as a basis the arguments that exegesis can
never contradict theology, and so Menahem's false linguistic
interpretations cause theological aberrations. By taking
philology as a basis for his exegesis, he considers that
Menahem is propagating dangerous heretical ideas.

118

Finally, Dunash openly states that he uses compared linguistics, unlike Menahem. The Mishna language, Aramaean and Arab, because of their great similarity to Hebrew, are going to throw light on complicated passages in the Hebrew language.

Dunash' *Hermeneutical principles* are:

First of all, the 13 *middot*, that is, the traditional exegetical rules used for writing on these subjects, and from which it is supposed that the Halakhical conclusions will be drawn. Dunash uses them very little in practice, and concentrates on exclusively philological aspects.

Secondly, the use of paraphrase, explanations to clarify obscure texts. In this case small additions or suppressions are sometimes allowed, or a change of words if necessary.

As a rule Dunash attempts to face up to various problems that Biblical interpretation stumbled on in the 10th. century:

- The determination of the radical or subordinate character of the letters in each term, so as to capture its meaning.

- The correct classification of the roots and their different meanings.

- The meaning of the *hapax legomena* (words which appear only once in the Biblical text), that present problems of interpretation, precisely because of not being able to compare them with other similar terms.

And Dunash tries to solve these problems in the following ways:

- Studying the context and similar passages in detail.

- Observing parallelism within the same passage.

- Resorting to everyday observance and common sense.

For example, in the case of the word *nidbakin* (Esd. 6,4) which Menahem interpreted as *walls,* referring to the construction of the second Temple. Dunash says:

"You have interpreted *nidbakin di `eben gelal telata* (there were *rows* of hewn stones...) (Esd. 6,4) in the sense of walls. Tell me, as a learned person, how can you build a house with three walls. Would you put one wall in front of the other, or with three corners? Is it not true that this later construction was similar to Solomon's first building, which was built with three rows of walls?"

- Putting his knowledge of morphology, accentuation and vocalization into practice.

- Using compared linguistics procedures.

MENAHEM'S DISCIPLES' TESHUBOT

Faced with Dunash' attack on Menahem's *Mahberet* three of his disciple launched a counter-attack. These disciples were Isaac ibn Capron, Judah ibn Daud and Isaac ibn Chiqatella.

On the lines of Dunash' *Teshubot,* they undertook a second series of Teshubot to defend their master as much from the linguistic as from the exegetic attacks which he had suffered.

As a prelude to the *Teshubot* themselves there is a poem dedicated to Hasdai, in the usual laudatory tone:

> *To the expert on the Sacred Books...*
> *The leader of Judah...*
> *Open up the streets,*
> *Make way*
> *For the faithful prince is coming...*

In the introduction in prose which follows, an insulting tone towards Dunash is adopted:

*In Dunash' heart envy and passion are rooted... His heart
has been led to sly plotting, imputing lies to Menahem ben
Saruq... He compounds treatise, sharpens his tongue,
talks nonsense, fills books with emptiness and wrong...*

In this introduction Menahem's disciples criticise
Dunash' metrical procedures and his attempt to apply Arab
versification to the Hebrew language. They go on to "reply" to
fifty five of Dunash' two hundred *Replies.*

Dunash has criticized Menahem sharply but within the
limits of a certain correction, now Menahem's disciples
attacked Dunash in a sarcastic and deprecating way, calling
him stupid, envious and arrogant. This tone, nevertheless,
would seem mild in comparison with the one Ibn Seset, a
disciple of Dunash', would later adopt on addressing himself to
them.

JUDAH IBN SESET'S TESHUBOT

The reaction of this disciple of Dunash' was not long in
coming; in defense of his teacher and the criticism levelled at
him by Menahem's disciples he wrote another series of
Teshubot refuting the former ones.

Ibn Seset wrote his *Teshubot* between 970 and 990 and
they would be published by S.G.Stern in 1870, nearly a
thousand years later.

According to Nehemia Allony, already mentioned, "there
is only news of one original text of this treatise and with the
only manuscript, which is conserved in Parma, confronting it
with Stern's edition, we have elaborated our study and edition
of the Teshubot."

Ibn Seset's work is made up of three parts:

- The first in metre, in which Dunash is praised, his opponents
insulted and an indication is given of the points which will be
referred to later.

- A brief introduction in rhyming prose as a prologue to the *Teshubot,* which is a chain of Biblical questions.

- The *Teshubot* themselves, forty one in all, that do not deal with all the questions debated by the authors of the previous Teshubot. In many of them he only repeats Dunash' arguments, quoting, as is the usual custom, Biblical texts to back his statements.

Let us see some of the introductory lines:

"He (Dunash) *turned the fools into an eloquent and brilliant people,*
The rash became cautious
And the drowsy into watchful...
His eyes drop humbly
When even princes and viziers
feel honoured by his poems...
I, a young disciple, will destroy his (Menahem's) disciples...
I will strike you, I will attack you,
I will make you drink bitter and poisoned waters..."

Then he mocks each one in turn, Ibn Capron because of his name, Ibn Daud, hinting at his possible Christian forms of exegesis.

In the grammatical field he brings out arguments that are really no more than misunderstandings, or even discusses purely formal questions, as in the case of the argument over the conventional terminology of "radical letters" and "subordinate letters".

On other occasions, however, Ibn Seset, following Dunash' lines, makes grave theological accusations of Caraism against Menahem and his disciples because of disagreements on linguistical questions, as in the case of the *teshubah lo'ra`ah.*

The dispute was not always so profound. Sometimes the controversy centred on problems of purely linguistic interest.

Chapter VI

THE RABBINICAL ACADEMY IN LUCENA (CORDOBA)

by FERNANDO DIAZ ESTEBAN*

1. WHY A RABBINICAL ACADEMY

In the same way that the Catholic religion is based on the New Testament plus the tradition of authority and interpretation known as the *Magisterium Ecclesiae* or *Teaching of the Church,* medieval Jewish religion is based on the written text of the Old Testament plus the group of rules and interpretations transmitted by the rabbis, and called the Oral law. In both cases, the principal foundation is the written law, the Sacred Scriptures. But a written text, as time goes by, cannot give concrete answers to the changing needs of a live community. For this reason new solutions must be found to new problems, trying to conserve the spirit and, as far as possible, the letter of the written law. Those in charge of carrying out the appropriate adaptations must, first of all, be familiarized with the written law and also with the interpretations and criteria their predecessors had proposed or imposed; in this way a live tradition has been created down the centuries, in which innovations are in keeping with the origin of the tradition itself.

---

*Professor of Hebrew Language and Literature. Barcelona Central University

Among the Jews, the experts in Oral Law are the Rabbis. Their authority is in direct proportion to their knowledge recognized by the community they serve and by the other Rabbis, with no relationships of discipline and ranking typical of priesthood.

Independently of a rabbi's personal prestige, his title confers him the recognition as expert in the Oral Law and so forming part of the tradition taught by Moses in Sinai.With the formula "from Moses in Sinai", the Jews trace the Oral Law right back to that same moment when Moses was entrusted with the Written Law in Sinai. In this way the Oral Law enjoys the same authority as the Pentateuch, for it was Moses himself who explained orally the principles that would serve to interpret and apply the written law. This is why special importance was attached to the continuity of the oral tradition, passing down from Moses' contemporaries to the Prophets, from the prophets to those who constituted the Great Synagogue, that is, the Jewish authorities after the Babylonian Captivity, and from the Great Synagogue members to the rabbis, who transmit from teacher to disciples generation after generation.

MISHNA, GEMARA, TALMUD

The first compendium of the Oral Law received the name of *Mishna* "repetition" of what was said by a rabbi to his disciples. It is important to point out that the *Mishna* is not a systematic code but an immense collection of discussions and opinions of the most famous rabbis between the 2nd. century B.C. and the 2nd. century A.D. The rabbis are presented arguing and offering different solutions to the same case, although later, one of the opinions prevails. When none of the opinions presented is recognized in the Mishna, the one to be followed is introduced by the formula "And the wise men say..." The way in which the Mishna presents the transmission of the Oral Law is very important, because it establishes the rabbis' freedom of opinion, with no limits other than that of

The Synagogue, Cordoba. Entrance.

The Statue of Maimonides in the Tiberiades Square in Cordoba's Jewish Quarter.

coherence with the tradition itself. This explains the disagreements between rabbis and the need to resort to the consensus of general opinion or the opinion of the authority who is admitted as being the wisest.

The Mishna, in turn, was established in a text, that had to be commented, explained and adapted to the new circumstances in life. This long drawn out adaptation lasted several centuries, from III to VI, and was written in Aramaean. It received the title of *Gemara* and was elaborated following the same technique of asystematic discussion from different points of view. The Mishna together with its Gemara is what was later known as the *Talmud* teaching. Maimonides, one of the pupils at the Lucena Academy explains the process like this:

> *After the tribunal of Rab Asy, the composition of the Talmud was completed in his son's time. Israel was dispersed throughout all the countries of the great Diaspore, reaching the limits of the earth and remote islands. Strife increased throughout the world, the ways were hampered by armies, the teaching of the Law decreased and Israel no longer went into the academies by the thousand to learn as they had done before. But chosen individuals called by God got together in every city and in every nation and they dedicated themselves to the study of the Law, delving into the works of the wise men and learning the Law method from them.*

> *Each tribunal constituted after the Talmud decreed, established orders and sanctioned customs for its respective nation, but they were not universally divulged throughout all Israel, because of the distance between settlements and the confusions on the roads; with a tribunal constituted individually for each nation and the Great Tribunal of Seventy having disappeared several year before, the Talmud was compiled. The people of one nation are neither obliged to follow the customs of another nation, nor will a tribunal dictate what another tribunal of the same nation must decree. So, if one of the gaons teaches a certain law procedure but a later tribunal interprets what is written in the Talmud in another way, there is no reason to follow the first, but the one whose*

opinion is better founded, either the first or the last. This with respect to sentences, decrees, orders and customs introduced after the Talmud was compiled, but all the words of the Babylonian Talmud must be followed by all the House of Israel and all the customs, decrees and orders adopted in every city and nation by the wise men in the Talmud prevail, as what is in the Talmud was adopted by all Israel and the wise men who established the orders, decreed, established uses, sentenced or taught legal procedure were all the wise men in Israel, or the majority, and had heard the whole tradition of the fundaments of the Law from mouth to mouth right back to Moses.

... All the scholars incorporated after the Talmud was compiled and who worked on it, and became famous for their wisdom, are called Gaons. All these Gaons who settled in Palestine, the country of Senar (Iraq), Spain and France, taught according to the Talmud, bringing its depths out into the light and making its subjects clear, for the Talmud method is very obscure and as it is in Aramaean mixed with other languages, a language clear enough for the inhabitants of Senar when the Talmud was compiled, but for the inhabitants in other places and for those of Senar in the Gaon's time it was unintelligible to all until it was taught.

Men in every city posed numerous questions to each of his contemporary gaons so that the difficult words in the Talmud could be interpreted and answered according to their knowledge. Those who asked collected the Responsa and compiled books which could be consulted. The gaons of each generation also compiled works to clarify the Talmud; some interpreted isolated halakot, others odd chapters which provided difficulties in their days; others, treatise and regulations. They also elaborated specific laws on what was prohibited and what was permitted, obligatory and free in matters which had to be available to those who were not able to delve into the depths of the Talmud. This is a divine task which all the gaons of Israel have undertaken since the day in which the Talmud was compiled right up to our days, which is the eighth year,

126

after the one thousand, one hundred posterior to the destruction of the Temple..."

PROFANE IMPORTANCE OF RELIGIOUS LAW

In Judaism no distinction is made between religious law and profane law. Everything has its justification and origin in religious acts. Both the Written and the Oral Law regulate not only religious beliefs and rites but also civil laws. Marriage, inheritance, commercial contracts, usury (prohibited); corporal and monetary punishment for delinquents; moral punishment (like ex-communion); all is regulated in the Talmud, or must be deduced from the Talmud so as not to deviate from the tradition which must be continued.

However, two ruptures with each tradition occurred, one religious and the other political.

The religious rupture was the destruction in the year 70 of the Temple in Jerusalem. This meant it was necessary to substitute the rites of blood sacrifices which were celebrated on the altar (oxen lambs or doves could not be killed now, nor could flour be burnt as stipulated offerings to God), so the caste of sacerdotal families, in charge of making sacrifices and looking after the Temple, no longer had any sense, as there was now no place to exercise their functions. The sacrifices were substituted by a series of prayers and the rabbis took over spiritual guidance.

The political rupture occurred when the kingdom of Judah disappeared; the Jews were submitted to civil and penal laws of other governors, based sometimes on other fundaments. In these cases the rabbis had to work out formulas which permitted the physical and spiritual survival of the Jewish people. They were lucky in that practically everywhere an ample juridical autonomy was conceded, with no other limitations that the general interest of state: payment of taxes, public peace and fidelity when faced with potential foreign enemies. This recognition of juridical autonomy for the Jewish community was corresponded by the rabbis with the aphorism *dina de malkuta, dina* "the law of the state is the law". Naturally the rabbis endeavoured to make the most of this aphorism, as the International Congress of Three Cultures in Toledo pointed out, and in any case, the communities always tried to obtain the maximum juridical autonomy. One of the communities that managed to do most was precisely that of Lucena.

2. WHAT WAS A RABBINICAL ACADEMY LIKE

That the rabbis be well prepared was a fundamental part in the contribution to a well-balanced community, for he not only provided religious but also juridical guidance and could estimate which non-Jewish governors' laws would be accepted or rejected and to what extent. A rabbi of prestige would gather around him disciples anxious to share his knowledge, or other experts would meet at his house to discuss obscure points. Rabbi Judah ibn Bile`am remembers meeting a man who came from Lucena and who told him that one day he had been at Samuel ibn Nagrella's son, Joseph's house in Granada, and that the wise men were sitting round Joseph interpreting the passage from Numbers XXII,7 "with fees in their hands". Although Joseph did not possess enough political ability to avoid the anti-Jewish revolt in 1066, organized by Abu Ishaq from Elvira, which resulted in the death of many hundreds of Jews including Joseph himself, he was still recognized as an authority in rabbinical matters, as this anecdote told by the traveller from Lucena confirms, and Abraham ben Daud is full of praise for him in his *Sefer ha-qabbalah* or "Book of (rabbinical) Tradition". Joseph studied Talmudism with his father, Samuel ibn Nagrella, in his own home, although it was more usual to attend an academy, a *yeshiva*, after having attended and shown progress at a *Beth Midrash* or "House of Study", normally annexed to every important synagogue.

The model for a rabbinical academy was that of the Babylonian academies and the description we have of them is impressive: the president enjoys the honourific title of Gaon (Excellency) and the vice-president and probable next in line that of *Av Beth-Din* (President of the Tribunal), responsible for seven chiefs of *Reshe Kalla* studies (chiefs of the Bride, alias by which the Academy was known), and the three *Haberim* (companions, colleagues). The commission or board of governors was composed by these ten *Allufim* (principals). Then there were thirty members who formed the equivalent of the Minor Sanhedrin, and finally, a hundred jurisprudence professors who made up the equivalent of the Great Sanhedrin.

Bearing in mind what we have said before, that religious and profane laws were united and mixed in Judaism, it is to be understood that the rabbinical academies also attempted to be a continuity of the last supreme tribunal that the Jews possessed when they still enjoyed autonomy in the Roman times of the Sanhedrin in Jerusalem. In the Adar months (February - March) and Elul (August - September) students used to come and hear the teachers and take the examinations . The Gaon presided this solemn session; opposite him sat the members of the Academy in seven rows of ten, according to the category of each member; the *reshe kalla* sat on the first row, behind the last row, the students. The session began with the statement by one of those seated on the first row of a question related to the Talmud treatise that had been studied in the previous session. The matter was discussed by those on the first row and, afterwards, by those seated on the other rows. When the matter had been fully discussed, the president summarized what had been said and gave the final verdict. At the end of the session, it was decided which subjects would be studied at home and these would be the object of discussion at the following session. The questions asked by the communities spread throughout the Diaspore were also studied, discussed and replies were given.

It is obvious that it cost a lot of money to maintain an academy, and the solution was to accept donations sent with the questions. One of the most important questions and its corresponding reply within the Jewish spiritual life was sent from Spain (it is supposed from Barcelona) to the Babylonian Academy in Sura. It was answered by Rabbi Amram Gaon, half-way through the 9th. century, that is to say, a century before the Cordoba Caliphate. It begins like this:

"Amram bar Sisna, president of the Academy in the city of Mahasia (Sura), to our teacher Isaac, son of our teacher Simon, beloved, esteemed and honoured by us and by the whole of the Academy. May heavenly peace and mercy be with you and with your descendants and with all the scholars and disciples and our brothers who reside there. Greetings from me and from R. Semah, the Ab Beth-Din (vice-president) of the Israel (Academy), and from the Allufim and from our learned men and students and from the city of Mahasia...Our teacher Jacob, son of our teacher Isaac, has given us the twenty gold pieces you donate to the Academy, five for us and five for the Academy's fund...And the Prayers and Blessings order for the whole year that you have requested, which has been taught by heaven; we have tried to organize and reply according to the tradition we have, as the tannaim set out (in the Mishna) and the amoraim (in the Gemara)..."

Then follows the order in which the prayers should be said and on which occasions. This responsa or reply is of great importance, because it was used as a guide by the communities in Spain and in practically all the Jewish world; on the other hand, Rabbi Smah is quoted quite frequently by two very important rabbis related to Lucena: Samuel ibn Nagrella and R. Isaac ibn Gayyat, president of the Lucena Academy for 38 years.

3. THE LUCENA ACADEMY

Naturally, the Lucena Academy suffered the upsets caused by the agitated times of the *Party Kingdoms*. Their scholars initially received the Cordoba and Granada tradition, and when decadence set in, its influence was prolonged through Abraham ben Daud and Meir ben Yosef ibn Megas, established in Toledo, and Abraham ben Maimon in Egypt. The list of illustrious visitors is long: Moses ibn Ezra, Judah Levi, Abraham ibn Ezra...

The history of Lucena has many spaces in blank. Hardly anything remains of what local tradition has as the synagogue and only one Hebrew tombstone has been found, although through literary references the epitaph on Alfasi's tomb is known. Cantera has studied what local scholars remember of the Jewish past in Lucena, from those who defend the possibility that it was founded by Noah's sons to those who believe in Nebuchadnezzar's fabulous arrival in Spain, accompanied by Jews. Some remember the Jews "in the town of Lucena had a University of Hebrew letters", but others not only deny this but also appear to ignore completely that there had been a Jewish *aljama* in this city. Baer includes the Jewish legend that Rabbi Natronai, gaon at the Babylo- nian Academy, jumped to Lucena, divulged the Torah and returned to Babylon in the same marvelous way, perhaps because Natronai says in his *responsa:* (Lucena) *is a place in Israel where many Israelites lived...and among you there are none of Gentile lineage...* The fact that the population of Lucena is exclusively Jewish is proverbial. Menahem ben Aharon ben Zarah states that all the city was Jewish in his book Provision for the Road. The Arab geographer, El Idrisi states also that all the city was Jewish and in the memories of the last Ziri king of Granada, Abd Allah, published by Levi-Provenal we read that the Moslems sometimes sent a military garrison. There was a responsible or chief of the Jews appointed by Abd Allah, called Ibn Maymun, who was father-in-law to Abu Rabi's son, treasurer to Abd Allah's grandfather; by chance, on undertaking certain repairs, part of the treasure hidden by the former treasurer was dis- covered ; Abd Allah sent for his son with the intention of making him confess where he had hidden the rest, but Ibn Maymun did not let his son-in-law travel to Granada and took advantage of the *taqwyya* or extra tax that the Granada king had imposed on Lucena and got the population to rebel. The general sent by Abd Allah to reduce them, Muammal, came to an agreement with Ibn Maymun that was not at all clear. Abd Allah appeared to agree but began to form a group of those dissatisfied with Ibn Maymun. When Ibn Maymun returned to Granada some time later, the Ziri king imprisoned him with the approval of those dissidents. Everything was fine between Lucena and Granada, according to Abd Allah, when in 1090 the Almoravids took

Lucena and deposed the Ziri. Dozy has taken from an Arab chronicle the news that a Cadi from Cordoba suggested to one of the Almoravide kings, Yusuf ibn Tasufin, that he demand the Lucena Jews to convert to Islam, as his forefathers had promised to Islamize if by the end of the 10th. century of the Hegira the Messiah had not appeared; the Jews were able to escape this measure, according to the chronicle, thanks to heavy bribes. After this respite, Jewish Lucena lived on until 1148 when it was taken by the Almohades and, like the rest of the Jews in Al-Andalus, the Lucena Jews were obliged to become Moslem or flee to save their lives. Cantera has published the elegy written by Abraham ibn Ezra on this occasion, which is really Lucena's epitaph, as it was never to regain its Jewish way of life nor its Academy.

Lucena had become a Jewish cultural centre that could rival Cordoba, but it was also a centre for commercial activity with its port of embarcation in Almeria. Among the letters written by Jewish traders in Arab, but with Hebrew characters, found in the Geniza in Cairo, S.D.Goitein refers to a letter sent to Lucena to the widely travelled trader Halfon ben Natanel in 1138. This great traveller maintained a close friendship with Judah Levi, although the former was an Egyptian Jew, perhaps partner in some business transactions , and sent payment by way of Judah ibn Gayyat, son of the first president of the Lucena Academy, Isaac ibn Gayyat, poet and friend of Judah Levi. In another letter published by Goitein, written and sent in 1141 from Fez to Almeria, among details of prices and state of markets, the occupation by the Almoravids from Sus is described, bad news made even worse by the death of *our teacher Joseph (ibn Megas), president of the Lucena Academy;* the writer expresses his enormous sadness because he had hoped to meet him personally and study under him. One of the "commercial" specialities carried out by the Lucena Jews was, according to Levi-Provenal, the castration of young captives to be used as eunuchs. However, letters from Jewish traders only mention textiles, wool, silk, metals, spices and food, and occasionally, paper and books. Although not related to Lucena, like the case we have described, traders informed each other of the death of some distinguished rabbi and expressed their sorrow, and this gives us an idea of the general feeling of respect towards the teachers of the Oral Law.

132

In the 9th. century there was already an outstanding scholar from Lucena in the person of Eleazar ben Semuel Hurga, who was famous in Babylon and was awarded the title of *alluf* of Spain *(de min Ispania)* and *rosh Kalla.* When Rabbi Moses settled in Cordoba and a rabbinical academy was established there, Spain became a rabbinical autonomy with respect to Babylon. Rabbi Hanok ben Mose succeeded his father in the Cordoba academy and was teacher to Samuel ibn Nagrella who, as we know, would later become vizier, poet and talmudist; Lucena is present in some of his war verses, such as the overthrowing of the attempted enemy siege and conquest of Granada in 1052 by a group of minor enemy kings, enemies led by the Seville *abbadíes.*

We have already seen how his son Joseph inherited his duties and fame, and at his house scholars met to discuss and learn juridical-religious matters. When he was murdered in the disturbances of 1066, his widow and son Azarias sought refuge in Lucena, under the protection of Isaac ibn Gayyat, who had studied with the Nagrellas in Granada as a youth. Ibn Gayyat even thought of leaving the presidency of the community to young Azarias, but he died very early on. Isaac ben Yehudah ibn Gayyat was born in Lucena in 1038, composed an elegy on the death of Samuel ibn Nagrella in 1056, in Aramaean, which is an indication of his keenness on talmudical studies, and in the elegy he expresses his wish for blessings for Joseph, Samuel's son. As a talmudical and rabbinical authority he wrote responsa to questions of a legal nature, partly conserved, plus legal compendiums on specialized subjects *Sa'are Simhat (halakot = laws),* explanations to the Kitab al-Siray Talmud and a commentary in Arab on the Book of Ecclesiasticus. Abraham ben Daud or David recounts how when he was mortally ill, he was taken to Cordoba so as to try and cure him, but he died and his corpse was transported to Lucena and he was buried there. His death was mourned by his many disciples, among them Moses ibn Ezra, Joseph ibn Sahl and Joseph ibn Saddiq. R. Joseph ben R. Yaaqod ibn Sahl, from an aristocratic family, with what he learnt at Lucena, was able occupy the post of Judge in the Cordoba community from 1113 to 1124, according to Ibn Daud, or till 1123, according to Moses ben Ezra. As an expert in Jewish law *(halaka),* he translated into Hebrew some of the responsa he had written in Arab by Isaac Alfasi, successor to Ibn Gayyat at the Lucena seat.

Another Lucena student, Joseph ben Yaaqob ibn Saddiq, born in Cordoba around 1076, was also a judge in that community from 1138 to 1149, year in which he died. As a philosopher he wrote a Neoplatonic *Microcosm* in Arab, and as a poet, he frequently made use of the *muwashshahat*. A contempor- ary of Ibn Gayyat was Isaac ben Baruq ibn al-Balia, from Cordoba, but of a family originally from Merida, a scientist at the service of the Seville *abbadíes*. Born in 1035, he composed an astronomical tract called *book* of *Intercalation* and dedicated it to Joseph ibn Nagrella in 1035; in 1069, al-Mutamid II (1040-1095) named him president of the Seville Jews and when he died in 1094, he was completing a rabbinical legal work titled *Quppat ha-rokelim* (The trader's basket); the three outstanding legal figures of that time, Ibn Gayyat, Alfasi and al-Balia disagreed on a certain question and this was to have a great effect on al-Balia's son, Baruc ben al-Balia, as we shall see further on.

R. Isaac ben Yaaqob al-Fasi (from Fez) was the person who gave the decisive backing to the Lucena academy. Alfasi was born in Kala Hamad (Morocco) in 1013; because of envy and personal enemies he had to flee to Fez and later to Cordoba in 1088 and, when ibn Gayyat died in 1089, he moved to Lucena as president of the academy. Lucena's prestige grew and as jurisconsultant has, as well as numerous responsa to legal questions, a synthesis of the Talmud call Halakot (Laws), in which, following the same order as the Talmud treatise, he presents definitive solutions, omitting the discussions, repetitions and names of rabbis that plague the Talmud. The next step would be taken by Maimonides, who orders the questions systematically according to subject matter and not treatise, but following the same spirit of synthesis and rationality as Alfasi. He died in Lucena in 1103 at the age of ninety and was buried there; his tomb- stone has not been conserved but we do have a copy of his epitaph, in which the great poet Moses ibn Ezra wrote a brief poem of six lines (*in this grave the fount of wisdom is buried,* reads one of them), followed by an extensive epitaph in prose.

The other outstanding figure from the Lucena academy was R. Joseph ben Meir ha-Levi ibn Megas. The surname Megas means "great" in Greek as we know, so it is possible that remote predecessors of his came from the Byzantine empire, either before or after the Moslems invaded Palestine. Because of disagreements with King Badis, his father, R. Meir, had to flee from Granada and take refuge in Seville. Joseph, born in 1077, was a disciple of Isaac ibn al-Balia who, according to Abraham ben David, *taught him day and night;* on al-Balia's death, he came to Lucena when he was twelve (1099) to study with Alfasi and, Abraham ben David says he *was at his side fourteen years studying day and night...(Alfasi) promoted him to rabbi before he died.* When he assumed the presidency of the Academy in 1103 it is natural that - in an atmosphere so charged with poetry and with Lucena so full of poets - one of them should dedicate a poem to him; none less than Judah Levi. Brody has published it and it is number 95 in the first volume. What a contrast between the sorrow expressed on Alfasi's death in the epitaph quoted earlier and the joy of the recent naming of his successor:

To Rabbi Joseph ha-Levi ibn Megas when he took the cathedral seat of his teacher, Rabbi Isaac al-Fasi.

My thoughts have been ordered today and give thanks to God for he is good.
See my eyes shine and my heart beats, a good thing.
And they fly towards my Lord for God has spoken well.
God also gives good things for he will not abandon my teacher.
And today I have truly learnt that my Lord is in our midst.
Awake, South wind, blow behind me, his aroma will be spread.
Blow on my spirit and improve the song of his graces
And reach Levi's harp and set its feet on the path to the poem
And his youthful days will return to serve the Lord.

135

Oh! all the thirsty and weary see that this is the Lord's encampment.
Go out and buy without money the religion renewed today
And Joseph will call it by law "up to this day"
This great mountain, "this Sinai" before the Lord,

You are truly the president of contentions Joseph, master in judicial
sentences.
Your God has lifted you up so that law and practice come alive and be admirable.
He has made your imagination agreeable a castle built on high.
So he has anointed you to be on the throne of our king, the Lord.

Today the strenght of truth has been imposed and justice has been maintained on its pedestal.
And the steps of the Torah feel proud and Glory has sat there forever.
And in your name authority has become great and piety has settled in its place.
You are its resolution and structure, you have been chosen by the Lord.

The waters and the dry lands will rejoice, and the mountains all together will shout for joy,
Your enemies will be covered in shame, and the tents of the wicked are no longer.
The words of his mouth and the expression of his lips and heart are pleasing
And in your name, the poem exalts: be blessed for the Lord's sake.

When Joseph ibn Megas died in 1141, *the world was bereft of the academies of wisdom,* says Abraham ben David. An unknown poet called Yequtiel dedicated an elegy to him, and we have just seen how a travelled trader lamented his death.

136

A son of Isaac ibn Baruc al-Balia, called Baruc ben Isaac al-Balia, born in 1077, received the tradition from his own father, but on his father's death and on his advice, he went to Lucena and told Alfasi that his father had pardoned him for the dispute they had had and asked Alfasi to forgive him too. Alfasi "adopted" young Baruc al-Balia intellectually and Baruc recognizes: *"I stayed, then, in his house and learnt all the Talmud with him"*. Baruc also studied what is known as Greek science, that is to say, sciences and philosophy , and among his disciples the youngest was Abraham ben David. Baruc died in 1126.

Lucena disappeared as a Jewish centre with the Almoravide invasion in 1148, until it was reconquered by Castile in 1240. When the anti-Jewish revolts broke out in 1391, they affected what was probably by now a scarce Jewish population in Lucena.

Joseph ibn Megas' son, Meir ben Joseph ibn Megas, and nephew Meir, passed from the Lucena rabbinical academy to Toledo, so Toledo became a sort of continuation to Lucena. Abraham ben David, disciple of Baruc al-Balia, also went there.

But Lucena's most famous pupil was Moses ben Maimon, Maimonides, disciple of Joseph ibn Megas, and he symbolizes the spirit of Lucena: knowledge of the Talmud, rational synthesis offering a direct solution, appreciation of sciences and philosophy and extensive knowledge of the Arab language.

Chapter VII

ON THE LIFE AND WORK OF MAIMONIDES

by DAVID ROMANO VENTURA*

INTRODUCTION

Mi-Moshe ad Moshe lo qam ke-Moshe. "From Moses to Moses there has never been another Moses", that is to say, from the Biblical Moses till Moses ben Maimon, Maimonides, the codifier of religious or Jurisdicial-religious laws, no other personality of such high intellectual stature existed in Judaism.

The sentence probably goes back to the first decades of the 13th. century, soon after Maimonides' death, and can be attributed to one of his followers in the disputes that confronted Maimonides' defenders and his detractors in Provence and Catalonia, disputes that had grave effects on occidental Judaism (and also oriental, but that is not within our present horizon).

Maimonides also enjoyed well-deserved renown outside Judaism. Thus, the Christian Church's scholastic philosophers within the Dominican trend, such as the German Albert the Great or the Italian Toms de Aquino (teacher in France) called

---

*Professor of Philology. Barcelona University.

Rabbi Moses of Egypt *Eagle of the Synagogue* and, to quote an example from Islam, the poet and author of literary precepts on khardjas, Ibn Sana al-Mulk (in Egypt) referred to him in verses which in a poor English translation would run:

> *Galeno's art only cures the body,*
> *Whilst Abu Imram's (Maimonides) cures body and soul.*
> *His knowledge made him the doctor of the century.*
> *With his knowledge he can cure the disease of ignorance.*
> *If the moon decided to put herself in his hands*
> *She would be freed of her spots at full moon.*
> *He would cure her of her monthly indispositions*
> *And prevent her waning in her moment of conjunction.*

These brief references serve to indicate or prove that Maimonides is not just a local or national figure, but enjoys international, or to be more exact, supranational relevance. In the same period, 13th. century, in different geographical, religious and cultural spheres in what we call

Europe and the Mediterranean world, leaders in all three religions had the highest esteem for Maimonides and, each in his own way, foresaw the part he was to play in the history of human culture.

1. SOME ASPECTS OF HIS LIFE

1135-1204 are the dates that enclose RaMBaM's life. RaMBaM is the name Jewish scholars have always afforded Rabbi Moses ben Maimon, following the tendency to acronimia, very frequent in designating rabbinical authors.

And between these two dates, almost seventy years, he lived entirely (there is little to back the hypothetical suggestion that Maimonides lived in the south of France, in Provence) in the Islam world, one of the three great blocks, Islam, Christian and Byzantine, into which the known world was then divided. That he was born and spent his childhood in Andalusian Cordoba, that for more than ten years he wandered round cities and regions of Al-Andalus (for certain Almeria at least), that he lived for five years in the Moroccan city of Fez and then moved definitely to Orient, all this really occurred in Moslem territory. After having lived a few months in the Palestinian Acre and another short spell in Egyptian Alexandria, in 1165 he settled permanently in Fostat, the old quarter of today's Cairo: what he had been preparing in those years of pilgrimage and unrest was to bear fruit here.

What were the consequences of having always lived in Dar-al-Islam, in the Moslem world? Many and diverse, perhaps too many to explain here. However, we cannot but mention at least some of them: a profound knowledge of the Arab language, being immersed in culture, whatever its originin culture expressed in the Arab language. To such a point that he wrote most of his works, and we shall come back to them, in Arab, but never with Arab characters but using the Hebrew alphabet, that is, he made use of an "aljamiado" Hebrew-Arabic or Arabic-Hebrew. This same resort had been used before and afterwards by many of his countrymen and fellow believers; to mention a few, Solomon ibn Gabirol ("Avicebron", held to be Christian by scholastic philosophers until the 9th. century, thanks to Munk) and Bahya ibn Paquda, Judah Levi and Moses ibn Ezra.

What explanations can we offer for this? The best I can think of is the following: references seem to indicate that Hebrew was then a language to be written and read, but not spoken. In other words, Maimonides' mother tongue must have been Arab, in one of its Andalusian varieties. But there is no doubt that explanations of certain subjects in Arab was ... dangerous, dangerous for their content (implicit or explicit) of Jewish truths. Using Hebrew characters, everything written in Arab was available only to Jews who knew Arab. Is this a valid explanation or could there be any other?

I must at this point briefly mention a question that is perhaps marginal but is important: on more than one occasion I have said and repeated that in the cultural field the Hispano Jews had a characteristic that afforded them superiority over Jews from European countries, and that characteristic was their knowledge of Arab, thanks to which the activity of translators from Arab to Latin is explained, with spoken

Romance as an intermediary; what is usually called "four hand translation". Twelfth century translators, of Maimonides' time, lived in territories where the Christian religion prevailed. I am referring to the so-called "'Toledo school of translators" (with the outstanding figure of Johannes Avendaut Hispanus), to contemporaries active in Leon, as well as in various cities in the Ebro Valley (Pamplona, Tarragona, Zaragoza, Huesca) and in Barcelona itself, as is the case of Abraham bar Hiyya.

Moreover, Arab dominance explains the activity, both then and later, of Jewish translators and leaders of the Arab section of the Crown of Aragon's chancellery, at least up until the end of the 13th. century, and it also explains the role of Jewish doctors in the peninsula states. All this without taking into account what Andalusian Jews emigrated to Lenguadoc translated from Arab to Hebrew; in this activity the Kimji and ibn Yibbon families were particularly relevant, and one of them, Samuel ibn Tibbon, would be the first to translate the *Moreh Nebukhim* (Guide of the Perplexed) as well as others of Maimonides' minor works. It is important to note that the Tibbonian translation was carried out in Maimonides' lifetime and with his approval and consent. The translations into Hebrew opened up the way to the diffusion of Peninsula Jewish culture among Jewish commu- nities beyond the Pyrenees, for Arab was really "Chinese" to non-Andalusians.

Let us get back to Maimonides. Because of the fanatical Almohade invaders, he was obliged to leave his native city and to leave it forever. That Cordoba described by the Moslem Idrisi, almost his contemporary, with shining colours and fiery passion at the same time as he lamented - I translate - that in the period in which we are writing this work, the city of Cordoba has been crushed by the mill-stone of discordance; the winds of fortune have changed her situation and her inhabitants have suffered enormous disgraces, and that is why the present population is so small. But even so, in all of Spain there is no other city with such renown. In an even worse state was the neighbour- ing Madinat-al-Zahra, that had been nothing but ruins for quite some time, but whose remains laid in situ; and we cannot discard the possibility that Maimonides had had occasion to contemplate them.

The *Almohade invasion* did not only provoke Cordoba's decadence, but, among other things, it marked the intellectual end of Andalusian Judaism. Contemporary poets captured this, like the wandering Abraham ibn Ezra, who dedicated an elegy to this theme (Qina), without much poetical value. Here are some verses:

Ay! Sepharad has been overwhelmed by a calamity from the skies;
My eyes, my eyes shed tears
Tears flood from my eyes, like fountains, for the city of LUCENA;
Unblemished, isolated, the captive community dwelt there
 unceasingly for one thousand and seventy years.
But its day came, its people fed and she was left like a widow,
An orphan with no Law, nor Scripture, the Mishna sealed,
The Talmud sterile, for she had lost her splendour.
Assassins and violent men run hither and thither;
The place for prayer and praise has been turned into a house for orgies.
So I weep and clench my hands and in my mouth there is always an elegy
And I never tire of saying: "Oh, If my head became waters"
Ah! Sepharad has been overwhelmed by a calamity from the skies:
My eyes, my eyes shed tears.

My head will grow bald and I will wail bitterly for the "aljama" in SEVILLE,
 for her wounded princes and her captured sons;
 for her daughters, so fair, handed over to a strange religion.

How was CORDOBA abandoned and turned into a sea of ruin?
There, the wise men and the great died of hunger and of thirst,

No Jew, not a single one, survived in JAEN, nor in
ALMERIA,
Nor in MAYORCA, nor in MALAGA did any any comfort
remain,
The Jews who fled were cruelly wounded.
So I lament bitterly and wail so much,
My cries flow like waters because of my grief.

Ay! Sepharad has been overwhelmed by a calamity from
the skies:
My eyes, my eyes shed tears.

Maimonides' biography should perhaps be re-elaborated
making intense use of his own explanations, declarations or
concepts. For example, I feel it is well worth reading an
autobiographical fragment referring to the long years spent in
Egypt and his medical activity there, as, because of adverse
circumstances, he had to earn his living practising medicine
daily during long and exhausting sessions:

I live in Fostat, while the Sultan lives in Cairo, at a
distance of two walks permitted on the Sabbath (about 5
kilometres). My duties at the Sultan's court are very
tiring. I must visit him daily, early in the morning; but
when he is feeling poorly or one of his children or one of
his concubines falls ill, I dare not leave Cairo, but have to
spend the greater part of the day in the palace. Very often,
one of two of his palace officials are ill too, and I have to
attend them during the day. So, normally, I travel to
Cairo in the morning and, all being well, arrive back at
Fostat after Lunch, starving, to find my waiting rooms
packed with people, Jews and nonJews, judges and
intendants, friends and enemies, a multicoloured crowd
waiting for my return.

I dismount, wash my hands and approach my patients,
entreating them to be patient while I have something light
to refresh me. Then I begin to attend my patients, writing
prescriptions and giving instructions for different
illnesses. Patients come and go until dusk and sometimes,
I can assure you, until up to two hours after sundown. I

talk to them and prescribe while laying back from sheer exhaustion. And when night falls I am so tired out that I can hardly speak.

As a consequence of all this, no Jew can talk to me nor discuss things with me except on the Sabbath. And then all the community, or most of its members, come to see me after the morning service and then I advise them on what they should do during the whole week; together we study a little, until midday. Then they leave. Some come back later and we go on reading until it is time for the evening prayer. And that is my daily life".

To complete these brief bibliographical allusions, I will refer for a moment to *Maimonides' appearance.* Let me make it quite clear that we do not have the slightest idea of Maimonides' physical appearance. But there are portraits... from the eighteenth century! In 1744 the Hebrew expert, Ugolino, in the first volume of his extensive collection of rabbinical materials, reproduced a medal about 5 cm. in diameter on which Maimonides' bust appears, with his name in Hebrew and in Latin, together with an inscription: *ex antiqua tabula.* This medal has inspired different graphical representations, each more elegant than the last, shaping and darkening his beard, and these have been reproduced in later editions of Maimonides' works, in several Jewish encyclopaedias and more recently in a Spanish book on Maimonides. Then followed an Israeli stamp (1953) and quite recently, a 1.000 *sheqalim* Israeli bank-note.

From one of these sources, but with free artistic interpretation, comes the sculpture in seated position conserved in one of Cordoba's tiny squares, inaugurated in 1964, and which is represented on the Spanish 1967 stamp.

Four details: 1st. The reproduction of this statue has been used profusely on material covering the 850th. anniversary of Maimonides' birth. 2nd. A large medal with a reproduction (taken from Ugolino's group) of Maimonides curing a child has been placed on the wall of Paris University's new Faculty of Medicine. 3rd. In the Washington Capitol are twenty three busts of great universal legislators, among them two Spaniards: Alphonse X, the Wise, and... our Maimonides. 4th. the Cordoba sculpture is engraved with the reproduction of one of the two auto- graphical signatures known to be by Maimonides.

2. MAIMONIDES' WORKS

Let us begin by remembering that he is the author of three quite extensive main works: *Guide of the Perplexed, Luminaria* and *Second Law,* the first two written in Arab although they are better known in their Hebrew version, while the *Second Law* was originally written by him in Hebrew. But in RaMBaM's work as a whole we must consider, and very much so, his briefer works, probably of less importance because they deal with specific subjects or questions, those called "punctual", although they cover quite a lot more than mere points.

Most *classifications of works* by any author runs the risk of omitting things. This problem has no solution but it is essential to face up to it. And I do so. Maimonides cultivated four main fields which can be classified (with the risks mentioned) as the following:

1st. *Philosophy*, not forgetting to include under this heading, or rather, to emphasize, theological questions, and in this sense perhaps it would be better, if it were not such an awkward word, to refer to Philosophical-theological works; a capital work, *Guide of the Perplexed.*

2nd. *Rabbinism*, that is, everything related to post-biblical Jewish religion, with the Mishna, the Talmud and the production derived from them, for example, dogmatic and liturgical subjects. In this field we must mention two great works: *Luminaria* and *Second Law.*

3rd. *Medicine.*

4th. *Astronomy,* with certain reservations in the use of this expression, as we shall now see.

As far as Maimonides' epistles and legal judgements are concerned, that is, what is usually referred to as *Responsa,* it is traditional to classify them in a separate group, with epistles and *Responsa* together as the limits that differen- tiate them are not at all clear. But with a peculiarity: each of them could be included, for better or for worse, in one of the four groups described before. Perhaps an example will make this clearer.

Asked by the rabbis in the south of France if *Astrology,* to believe in astrology, was compatible with the principles of the Jewish faith, Maimonides answered in a letter, not a *responsa,* that believing in astrology could be compared with idolatry, underlining that astrology *"based on the influence of the stars, is not a science at all, but pure foolishness... which deserves to be ignored".* According to his opinion this pseudo-science must be distinguished from the truly scientific astronomy. But, in passing, he recognizes that astrology was the first "science" that he studied; explain- ing that in his youth he read all the astrological tracts available in Arab. That is to say, quite a substantial technical question is dealt with in a mere letter.

Before going into details of Maimonides' work, it is convenient to remember that as well as his contemporaries, Jewish and Moslem (but not Christian), the whole fund of Greek knowledge was available to him, revealed and transmitted by scholars who wrote in Arab. And all this in three of the four fields where he exercised his intellectual activity; it is only in rabbinical questions where he depends exclusively on Jewish authors.

Other chapters have referred to Maimonidian philosophy so I will limit myself to a few observations only. The first is the question of the title of his most important work: *Guide of the Perplexed,* in my lectures I avoid using the article in Spanish fearing the decision of making it masculine or feminine. In Arab the word guide is feminine *(Dalalat al-ha'irin),* whilst in the Hebrew translation, the title, apparently given by

147

Maimonides himself, is masculine *(Moreh Nebukhim)*. In French, there is no problem as both meanings of "guide" are expressed by the same gender - masculine.

Perhaps it would help to remember that the medieval Spanish translation, XV century and as yet unpublished, by Pedro of Toledo - the second part was completed in Zafra in 1419, the third in Seville in 1432 - says that *Moreh quiere dezir mostrador e ensennador de los turbados (Moreh* means showing and teaching the confused). If we accept this idea, it would be better to say in Spanish *El guía de perplejos.*

I must (must or want to?) remind readers that this work was translated in RaMBaM's own lifetime, less frequent than that today. Obviously the possible number of readers affected by this question was quite high. For this reason RaMBaM says that *the object of this tract is not to make (the meaning of words that appear in prophetical books) understandable to common people, beginners... or to those who are only concerned with our sacred law... The object is to explain to religious men, educated in the belief of our Holy Law, who comply faithfully with moral and religious duties, and at the same time have followed philosophical studies... and who finds it difficult to accept as correct the teaching based on literary interpretation of the Law... and for this reason is sunk in perplexity and confusion."*

Voices undoubtedly more authorized than mine could describe Maimonides' *medical production,* that covers no less than ten tracts, although some of them are quite short. The original texts - in Arab, remember - of five of them lie unpublished on the shelves of European libraries, while the Hebrew versions have found better fortune - or interest - and almost all of them have been published.

Translations into Latin (usually from Hebrew and not from the Arab original), date from the 13th. century and with the first days of the printing press were soon known throughout the West. Readers (doctors) who lived in the 15th. and 16th. century were able to study Maimonides' medical ideas on good health: his *De regimine sanitatis* was published and republished several times, as were his observations on hysteria expressed in a tract that has the unprepossessing and perhaps cryptic title of *Explanations of the causes of apparent accidents*, while his study On poisons and their antidotes and *Study of Asthma* probably never went any further than Jewish circles. : they were translated into Latin but never published. So we can assume that very few people read them.

But medical subjects did not stop here; Maimonides commented maxims by great doctors from ancient Greece by Hypocrates and Galeno, abridged some of their works and even dared - I am joking when I say "dared" - to make a collection of his own maxims, 1500 of them! And what is more, in answer to a request by a nephew of Saladino, wrote some physical and moral observations on copulation and, always in Arab, a tract with seven chapters on haemorrhoids: his bibliography has repeated, and goes on repeating, erroneously of course, that these pages on haemorrhoids were translated into Spanish with the delightful title "Sobre los Milagros" (About Miracles)!

A large part of these works appear to be - and are! - the result of personal experience in medical practice, as he explains himself in a letter to his favourite disciple - Joseph ibn Shamun -: *you well know how difficult is this profession for a conscientious and meticulous person who only affirms what he can prove with arguments or with authority.* An important text, and the following too: *Medical practice is not knitting or weaving or manual work, but must be felt from the heart, be full of comprehension and doted with the gift of keen observation. These qualities, together with a correct medical knowledge, are indispensable requisites for competent medical practice.*

The text quoted earlier, in which he describes a day's work, refers to this medical practice. And one more observation, according to Maimonides, medicine, real medicine, is, or should be, threefold: preventive medicine, curing the patient and the following up of the convalescent (including invalids and the elderly).

Maimonides' *astronomy* is reduced in fact to two works: one on *the Jewish calendar* and another called *Rules for the consecration of the new moon,* which deals precisely with fixing the beginning of the month on a calendar like the Jewish one which is based on observation of the new moon during twelve or thirteen months, one of which marks the beginning of the

149

year. That is to say, in other words, an astronomy that is "ancilla theologiae", which serves to determine and comply with a religious activity. And, nevertheless, Maimonides occupies a well-deserved place in the history of astronomy, even though this tract has not always enjoyed an independent existence but was included in the vast *Second Law* I shall refer to in a moment.

It is far from my intention to exhaust this subject but. I will say that precisely in the *Second Law* comes a descript- ion of an astronomical instrument, the sun-dial, of which various Andalusian examples have survived, one of them in the Archaeological Museum in his native Cordoba. This one is a sun-dial with Arab inscriptions; Maimonides holds that it is licit to resort to works carried out and written by nonJewish astronomers.

And so we come to the last of the fields cultivated by Mainmonides: *Rabbinism,* where strictly rabbinical works can be included, but also letters and *responsa* that deal with similar subjects.

Maimonides is unique in this case, too, for reasons that could be classified as casual or, at least, beside the essential point of the question. I have no knowledge of any author - I am not saying they do not exist, but that I do not know of any other Jewish author from the medieval Jewish period whose autographical texts have survived, with at least two signatures, one of that has been amply divulged for more than a century beginning or ending with the Cordoba sculpture, while the other signature has been relegated to a very modest secondary role and I must confess that I have not actually seen its original. Each of them appears on works belonging to this same rabbinical group but another difference exists between them: the well known signature on the *Second Law* manuscript and its complete text runs: (this copy) *was corrected in my book. I, Moses, son of Rabbi Maimon - blessed be his memory -*. The other is to be found in a fragment, all of it autobiographical, that comes from the Cairo *genizah.*

I must explain: the Hebrew word genizah refers to the lumber-room adjoining a synagogue and in which books and other written texts are deposited so as to avoid the profanation of God's name that appears in them. The best known of the *genizah* is that of Fostat's old synagogue in Cairo, discovered mid-nineteenth century. And it is well famous thanks to an exceptional condition: Egypt's very dry climate that permitted the texts to remain in a relatively good state of conservation for almost ten centuries. Among these texts, distributed today throughout the great deposits of manuscripts stored in Cambridge, Oxford, Lenningrad - also in London, New York, Paris etc. -. and many other texts of diverse character, there are quite a lot of Maimonides' signatures. In other words, the great majority of Rambam's autographs come from this *genizah* in Cairo. There are only two exceptions: the work with the signature referred to before and the volumes that make up one complete work, *Luminaria,* but are distributed among various owners that I cannot be precise about as some of these volumes, that belong to individual persons, have been sold or are sold today in public auction in aid of charitable institutions.

As well as other minor works, RaMBaM wrote two important rabbinical works; first, a commentary on the Mishna (in Arab *Sirach,* in Hebrew *Sepher ha-maor*), which translated means Luminaria, that was completed in 1168, and secondly,a Mishna codifier completed in 1180: the *Mishneh Torah* or Yad ha-hazaqah, or *Second Law,* written directly in Hebrew and in a Hebrew generously praised by later Jewish scholars. So, each of these works was completed during his long stay in Egypt, but it is to be supposed that they were conceived earlier - in the first case we know for sure that it was begun in 1158 -. Both *Luminaria* and the *Second Law* are exceptional works, of extraordinary importance, extremely systematic and perhaps for this very reason they have not been sufficiently studied - for the moment.

The *Luminaria* was translated into Hebrew by the efforts of six authors; we have here an indication of the difficulties it presented for a single translator. Completed in 1298, almost a century after Maimonides' death, this Hebrew translation had little or relatively little diffusion to judge by the reduced number of manuscript copies that have reached us and by the fact that only one complete Hebrew edition has been published (in Naples, from 1492 on). To tell the truth, Judaism has preferred Rashi's commentary, earlier, more didactical, if less profound that RaMBaM's *Luminaria.*

As far as the *Mishneh Torah* or *Second Law* is concerned, dedicated to Jewish believers, who are perplexed as they have no knowledge of philosophy, it is what we call in rabbinical terminology "codification", that is, a system- atic , reasoned or reasonable classification of jurisdicial matters scattered about the Talmudical ocean. A more complete codification than others (as even laws not valid outside Palestine are taken into account), and better than the others, although it only occupies the fourth or fifth position in distribution ranking. Bearing in mind the difficulties involved in penetrating the vast ocean of the juri-religious production of post-biblical Judaism,

> *I, Moses ben Maimon, the Sephardi, trusting in God - - Blessed be his name! - decided to study all those works and make a collection of all the results of what is prohibited and what is permitted, what is pure and what is impure, and all the other rules, so that all the Oral Law could be learnt systematically and without difficulties... and I titled this work Second Law with the end in mind that any who study the Written Law and later this work, would know the Oral Law entirely.*

This work justifies or explains the presence of Maimonides among the twenty three great legislators commemorated in Washington's Capitol.

Among his *minor rabbinical works,* minor in extension and relevance, written in Arab, we can find commentaries on Talmudical tracts, a great deal of them unpublished and whose authenticity has aroused reasonable doubts. But three of these minor works have enjoyed a double life; one as part of the major works and another independent life. So, the *Eight Chapters* or *Book of the Soul,* translated into Hebrew under the title of *Shemona peraqim* or *Sefer ha-nephesh* in Maimonides' lifetime (in 1202), was introduced into the liturgy, to be exact, into the Italian and Greek rites, in the 14th. century and perhaps earlier.

On the other hand, the *Book of Precepts* and the *Thirteen principles* were amply accepted by Judaism in their Hebrew

152

version. The *Book of Precepts* represents the best systematization of the 613 precepts in Judaism, which are classified in two main groups: 248 positive and 365 negative, while the *Thirteen principles* have become basic dogma, if this term can be used, in Judaism. They are the declarations of faith, the *Shelosha eser iqqarim* that a practising Jew recites at the end of the morning prayer, beginning: *ani ma'amin be-emuna shelema she-ha-bore - yitbarak shemo - hu bore u-manhig le-kol ha-beru'im, we-hu lebado asa we-ose we-yaase le-kol ha-ma-asin, (I believe with complete faith that God - blessed be his name - is the creator and guide of all creatures and only He made, makes and will make all things that are created).*

I have taken quite a time to mention or explain only a few of the many things that can be said about the life and work of Maimonides. But much more time would be necessary to mention everything. Custom can often lead to abuse and I have no intention of abusing my readers' patience.

Ergo: finally a few closing words about an author, Maimonides, bilingual, but seriously and not superficially, who uses two languages, Hebrew and Arab, but one graphical system: Hebrew; who was appreciated, although in different degrees by Christians, Jews and Moslems and is remembered today in Christian Cordoba, one time Al-Andalusi, illustrating the saying: "From Moses to Moses, there has never been another Moses".

BIBLIOGRAPHIES

Abraham ben David, *Sepher ha-Qabbala.* Translated by Jaime Bages, Granada 1921, in "Revista del Centro de Estudios históricos de Granada y su reino" XII (1921) 105-178, Valencia 1972.

Abumalham, M., *Edición, traducción y estudio del Kitab al-muhadara wa-l-mudakara de Moshe ibn Ezra.* Madrid 1982, 2 vols.

Aguilar, M./Robertson, I., *Jewish Spain. A Guide*, Madrid 1984.

Amador de los Ríos, J., *Historia social, política y religiosa de los judíos de España y Portugal*, Madrid 1973. (Reimp. of 1st. edition,1875).

Ashtor E., *The Jews of Moslem Spain.* Philadelphia 1973-1979, 2 vols.

Atienza, J.G., *Guía judía de España*, Madrid 1981.

Aviva Doron, *Yehudah ha-Levi. Repercusión de su obra.* With a *Semblanza de Yehudah ha-Levi* by Díaz Esteban, F., Barcelona 1985.

Baer, Y., *Historia de los judíos en la España Cristiana*,Madrid 1981,2 vols.

Baron, S.W., *Historia social y religiosa del pueblo judío*, Buenos Aires 1968, vol.VII.

Cahen, C., *El Islam*, I, (Historia Universal Siglo XXI), Madrid 1968.

Cantera Burgos, F.,*La judería de Lucena*, "Sefarad" XIII (1953) 343-354; *Lápida hebraica opistógrafa de Lucena*, "Sefarad" XIX (1959) 137.Cantera F./Millás Vallicrosa, J.M., *Las inscripciones hebraicas de España*, Madrid 1956.

Carmi T. (Ed.), *Hebrew Verse* (The Penguin Books),USA 1981.

Castillo, R., *Antología. Cuatro poetas hebraicoespañoles*, Madrid 1973.

Del Valle, C., *La escuela hebrea de Córdoba*, Madrid 1981.

Díaz Esteban, F., *Literatura hispanohebrea*, in Díez Borque J. M.,*Historia de las literaturas hispánicas no castellanas*, Madrid 1980, 179-219; *Aspectos de la convivencia jurídica desde el punto de vista judío en la España medieval*, II Congreso Internacional Encuentro de las Tres Culturas, Toledo 1983.

Díez Macho, Alejandro, *Moshe ibn Ezra como poeta y preceptista*, Madrid 1953.

García Iglesias, L.,*Los judíos en la España Antigua*, Madrid 1978.

García Villada, Z., *La cuestión judía durante la época visigoda* "Razón y Fe" 99 (1932)145-162.

Gil J., *Judíos y cristianos en la Hispania del siglo VII*: "Hispania Sacra" 30 (1977) 1-101.

Goitein, S.D., *Letters of Medieval Jewish Traders*. Translated from the Arabic with Introduction and Notes, Princepton University press 1973.

Gonzalo Maeso, D.,*Manual de historia de la literatura hebrea*, Madrid 1960; *El legado del judaísmo español*, Madrid 1972; *Guía de Perplejos*, Madrid 1983.

Millás Vallicrosa,J.M., *Literatura hebraicoespañola*, Barcelona 1967; *La poesía sagrada hebraicoespañola*, Madrid/Barcelona 1948;*Shelomó ibn Gabirol como poeta y filósofo*, Madrid/Barcelona 1945.

Navarro Peiro, A./Vegas Montaner, L., *Los poetas hebreos de Sefarad, capítulo III del Tahkemoni de Al-Harizi*:"Sefarad"

XLI (1981) 321-338; *La poesía hebrea, capítulo XVIII del Tahkemoni de Al-Harizi*: "Sefarad" XLII (1982) 140-171.

Pérez Castro, F.,*Aspectos de la cultura hebraicoespañola*, Santander 1964.

Romano, D., *Biografía de Maimónides* and *Las Obras rabínicas de Maimónides*, in *Maimónides y su época*, Córdoba 1986,16-31 and 50-65.

Romero E., *Shelomo ibn Gabirol, Poesía Secular*, Madrid 1978.

Sáenz- Badillos, A., *Los judíos en la historia y la cultura de la Andalucía medieval*, Granada 1980; *En torno al Mahberet de Menahem ben Saruq* in "Miscelánea de Estudios Arabes y Hebraicos" XXV,2 (1976) 11-50; *Teshubot de Dunash ben Labrat*, Granada 1980; *La hermenéutica bíblica de Dunás ben Labrat*, Simposio Bíblico Español, Madrid 1984.

Sotomayor, M., *Andalucía no es Al-Andalus*, "Proyección" XXX (1983) 133-145.

Varela, M.E., *Teshubot de Yehuda ben Seset*, Granada 1981; *Las bases de la gramática hebrea moderna* in"Sefardica 2", (1984) 89- 98.

Weinberger, L.J., *Jewish Prince in Moslem Spain*. Selected Poems of Samuel ibn Nagrela,Alabama 1973.

***

GLOSSARY

Aggadah (or **haggada**). The Section of the Talmud and Midrash containing homiletical expositions of theBible, stories, legends, folklore or maxims etc. as distinct from the *halakhah*, concerned with rabbinic law.

Aljama. Name to designate the Jewish community living in a Christian town; sometimes used synonimously for *Judería*.

Askhenazi. German, West-, Central-, or East-European Jews and their descendants.

Beth Din. Rabbinic court of law.

Beth ha-midrash. A school for higher rabbinic studies, often attached to a synagoge.

Dayan ("judge"). Member of rabbinic court law.

Diáspora. A reference to the dispersion of the Jews; a Jew living outside Israel.

Diwan (Arabic). A collection of poems or literary works by one author.

Gaon (pl. **ge'onim**, "eminence"). Title of the heads of rabbinic academies, especially in Babylonia, from the sixth to the eleventh century.

Gemara. The specific term for the discussions carried on in the rabbinic academies in ancient Palestine and Babylon on the *Mishna*, and together with the Mishna constitute the *Talmud*.

159

Genizah. Depository for used and damaged Hebrew manuscripts and books.

Halakhah. The sections of rabbinic literature concerned with religious, ethical, civil and criminal law.

Judería. The sector of a town inhabited by Jews: see Aljama.

Kabbalah. Jewish mystical tradition, originating in Provence in the thirteenth century.

Karaites. Schismatic sect, originating in the eight century, which accepts only the biblical tradition and rejects rabbinic authority.

Khardja (Arabic). The concluding lines, usually a couplet,of a *muwashshah*.

Kina (pl. **Kinot**, "lament"). Dirges recyted on days of mourning.

Ladino. Spanish-Jewish dialect, used as an everyday language by the *Sephardim*.

Maqama (Arabic).Narrative in rhymed prose, interspersed with metrical poems.

Masora. Notes entered on the top, bottom, and side margins of the Jewish Bible to safeguard the traditional transmission.The Masoretes were the scribal preservers of the Masora.

Midrash (pl. **midrashim**). Rabbinic method of biblical Exegesis, also collections of such homiletical interpretations or legal discussions.

Mishna. Earlierst codification of Jewish Oral Law, edited by Judah Hanasi (d.225 C.E.). which forms the basis of the *Talmud*.

Mozárabe. Term denoting a Christian living under Moorish rule.

Muwallad or **Muladí.** A Christian converted to Islam.

Muwashshah (Arabic). Metrical strophic poem ("girdle poem") which regularly alternates lines with separate rhymes and others with common rhymes.

Paytan (pl. **paytanim**). Liturgical poet.

Pentateuch. The five books of Moses: Genesis, Exodus, Leviticus,Numbers, and Deuteronomy

Piyut (pl. **piyutim**). Liturgical poem.

Qasida (Arabic). Non-strophic poem, employing quantitative metre and uniform rhyme.

Rabbi. One learned in the Mosaic law; hence a teacher of the law.In Modern Judaism the rabbinate is an ordained office.

Sephardim. Spanish and Portuguese Jews and their descendantswherever resident, as distinct from *Askhenazim*.

Sepher Torah. Manuscript scroll of the *Torah*.

Shema ("hear!"). Judaism'confession of faith, proclaiming the absolute unity of God (Deut. 6:4) (Shem-Israel Adonai Elohenu Adonai Ehad)

Sheol. Underworld.

Talmud. Collection of rabbinic discussions completed c. the sixth century which forms the basis of Jewish Oral Law.

Torah. The first five books of the Bible.

Yeshiva (pl. **yeshivot**). Traditional academy for the study of rabbinic literature.